Become Wise
or
Wounded

Anthony Dunne

Shield Crest

Copyright 2020 Anthony Dunne

All rights reserved

ISBN: 978-1-912505-86-9

MMXX

A CIP catalogue record for this book
is available from the British Library

Published by
ShieldCrest Publishing,
Aylesbury, Buckinghamshire,
HP18 0TF, England
Tel: +44 (0) 333 8000 890
www.shieldcrest.co.uk

This book is dedicated to my late mother
Joan Mangan

ACKNOWLEDGMENTS

Special thank you for the support of my son Aaron revile, Sandra Camargo and Carmel Tierney who kindly helped with proof reading.

CONTENTS

INTRODUCTION

Welcome to my book.

I say "my book" but it's actually more of a conversation.

I don't claim to own any of this, no more than I own the English language, for isn't everything we've learnt in life merely 'impressions' of what we've accumulated along the way. I barely went to school when I was a child - it was a different world back then.

College or university were not on any radar for me or for many of my friends at that time, nor was the idea encouraged. I knew no one that was set on education after secondary school. As time passed that all changed as I was soon to realise education helped to broaden our minds, it opened the cookie jar and some of the fruits of life come much easier with credentials.

So, as an adult I decided to get myself a few degrees although I'm not sure if I was satisfying some form of ego, inner self-belief, curiosity or the pure challenge of it all. I always felt that true intelligence was problem solving but while debating this subject with my wise neighbour Carmel Tierney, she concluded that intelligence was the ability to learn and I agree, so it does not matter what your history is, what family or background you came from, we all have huge ability.

The world was changing quickly and I knew I must adjust and keep changing also, for those that have the ability to change do proper.

We all want more, that's for sure and life can truly be a wonderful journey. As the famous proverb says - a journey of a thousand miles begins with a single step - but it also starts with an intention. Just like taking that first step, pushing from the hips forward to create momentum, we must also be aware of the direction in which we are going.

The big question for most people in life should be, why are we here and where are we going?

The truth is that none of us truly know our destination. It has been said by many people that we are here to grow and yes, I sit in that camp too and that's what we will discuss in finer detail here as we flow with these pages.

We are here to look at ourselves, to identify and to move past our attachments, fears, beliefs, identities and the ego, in order to self-actualise our awareness in to our own consciousness.

All big words perhaps I sense muttering in the shadows but, if I could corral them all into one camp...... Fear plays a huge part.

Our entanglement with fear blocks people from changing their intention at the deepest level.

The true intention of a person is at the heart of everything.

When we realise that everything in life is not about us, yes me too, and realise it's about others being an equal inclusive part of everything, this is the basis of growth. If you are focused only on yourself, self-absorbed, growth may be slow, as you are only interacting with your own self.

The journey involves an inclusive interaction with all of life.

When I say interaction and giving, I am not talking about a transaction, where I give and then I receive back, somewhere down the line - that's not giving.

You must give wholeheartedly. This must be your true intention.

Before you switch off and start thinking you may have to change your life, you don't!

No need to sit on top of a mountain or stop doing anything at all!

You can still be the unique, interesting and the crazy person you wish to be. Everything you have to learn in life is right in front of you and available to you in this moment.

As humans we can be sceptical of people bearing gifts but there is no catch here, all you have to do is observe and monitor your intention and this awareness. This has a knock-on effect which heightens your ability to also recognise the intentions of others.

These are the choices you can choose to make.

~1~

Choices

L et's start and go forward with a simple example.
If someone says something rude to you today, you
have choices - to respond or not, to become angry,
to walk away dismayed and allow it to upset your day - or
you could recognise that the person is truly only unhappy
in themselves, for isn't that why they are acting in such a
dramatic way.

Now that you have this information, you have a choice
to help them or not.

We all have many interactions with people daily....by
monitoring our own traps, we can strengthen our
awareness and we are less likely to fall for these traps
that could hinder our own growth.

We grow when we convert these into our deepest and
innermost feelings, its then we can integrate this in a
healthy way and genuinely help others.

This is evolving, evolvement of the human spirit and
whether we're dragged in that direction or try to ignore it,
continues growth is our direction.

Letting go of fear takes courage. It involves getting to
a point where, whatever happens your able to say, 'I will,
you/me/us will deal with it with 100% good intention.

This leaves the fear dead in the water and this
courage is programmed into everyone's DNA.

The worst scenario, which I've observed in many
spiritual and/or religious people, is, when someone is
only pretending to be in this state but does not truly

believe it at their deepest level, there will be little or no effect and very little growth.

This action may fool others, but you can't hide from your own true self or your life's journey. This will be mentioned many times in this book. Yes, you must lose the attachment to control. Life is full of many variables. Control is only fear. Our default position is survival, you don't need to live in that state. These are your choices and decisions people make. You can make them today or you can ignore them entirely, either way you have the freewill to do so.

Sadly, people think they can control certain parts of their life; relationships, family, jobs, etc but the only thing you can control is yourself! Let control go and deal with whatever situations come up.

Life isn't what happens to you - it's how you deal with it, that's evolvement in a nut shell.

I could finish this book at this point as, when we let fear go, life becomes joyous - things will never upset you to the same extent again. As this is a big subject, I know there will be some hardliners listening to or reading this so....... like building a sculpture, we can chip away at it and see what we have created in the end.

For now, allow everyone you are in contact with to be a teacher and a lesson for you. If you are taking the position of thinking that you know it all, then the ego is clearly controlling you.

Living life gracefully with the uncertainty of what life brings - that's part of the journey.

When we stop trying to control life then we start to truly learn we are on the correct path.

Many people simply cannot deal with the uncertainty of not knowing. They want to label it and put it in a box as they feel it is then resolved. Just stay open minded and don't take the bait, or any position at all, remain an open-minded observer. Taking a position cuts ourselves off from evolving and growth as it rules out all the other huge possibilities.

Repeatedly ask yourself the big question, what is my mind, body and soul intention in all I think, speak, and do? Examine closely the motivations of the intention for everything you do, think or say.

For instance, am I thinking of only me or in an inclusive way for all?

We are all just like water in the ocean; we cannot separate ourselves from each other, for we are all equal parts of one great ocean.

As the great Bruce Lee once said,

"Knowing is not enough, we must apply. Willing is not enough, we must do".

~2~

Beliefs

While growing up in a small village, religious beliefs were a big part of life. They were intertwined with everything else: connected with schools, politics, holy days, funerals, christenings, confirmations, communions and so on.

I smile from time to time as I can still hear the father figure in our house waking everyone up for Mass with military precision and every now and then you would get the speech, *"As long as you live in this house you will go to "Mass"*

This was the Sunday ritual and rather than challenge it, my siblings and I would comply and go to church like cows being lulled at milking time. So, we would wait outside the church, like savants protesting against their master....

At an early age I questioned everything, sometimes to my own detriment.

What were all these beliefs about? Doesn't it mean that people believe something to be true?

And when we believe something to be true, it seems to give us a feeling of confidence because we know something and have attached ourselves to this belief, this offers a sense of security and sureness. But haven't we seen confidence and stupidity go hand in hand, which can be a dangerous combination.

Holding on to these beliefs, people may feel they know something rather than accepting that they know very little and have so much to learn.

We only have to look briefly at our history and all the beliefs written about other humans that we frown upon today. But at that time, they believed 100% they were right, master races, slavery, religious wars and so on, all illusionary and they were also confident, for the most part they thought that what they believed was right. It is all disapproved now but it still goes on at different levels, all unfounded beliefs.

When we start looking closely around us and the world we live in, we should clearly understand that we know only a minuscule amount about what is truly going on. If I was to ask five people to look at a painting, I would get five different interpretations of what they saw. So why would I accept anyone's view on anything without looking at it myself? Or why would I accept information in a religious book by an author I've never met, or have no knowledge of any of it is true.

This goes for all beliefs worldwide. You see, what you believe dictates how you think, what you think becomes an emotion, an emotion then dictates what you feel, do or don't do in life, these are always aligned then the results just reinforce these initial belief, so....people get caught in their belief cycle. This is a choice people are making, but here's the money shot as they say. If you believe something is true but if it's not in your experience this is a form of illusion and one of humanity's biggest traps and failures.

As a teenager in the 80s, I've fond memories of a time with less technology, great music, just two TV channels and the internet was only an idea in someone's mind. But even then, there were soap operas and gossip and dramas happening everywhere, young and old, male and female all participated in the ongoing sagas and sequels. The more shocking the information, the greater the effect it had or the attention it gained, like fuel on the fire, and it gained momentum quickly with each event and everyone filled up on it.

At this point I realised everyone had difficult situations happening in their lives, but I also realised some people gained wisdom from those situations whilst others became wounded.

I stood in the camp where, if terrible things happened to you, you ought to have grown wiser....

In our house, sympathy was not a given so you quickly moved on from any event that had happened. We all remember as a child falling down, you could quickly pick yourself up and learn from it and never do it again.......... fire burns, animals can bite and hurt and so on.

If the worst possible events befall you, you could be the wisest of them all as you have that in your experience.

For isn't all experience a form of knowledge and information?

However, instead of growing wise, some people became wounded.

Rather than using this situation, however ugly as an opportunity for growth,

Unfortunately, they use it as an opportunity to say,

I am the way I am because of someone else or an event that happened to them.

This is using life's situations merely as an opportunity for self-destruction or stagnation.... So hence they have not become wise but wounded.

I didn't buy in to this victim stuff one bit, I had no willingness to find myself trapped by anything. I wanted to be free of traps.

As a kid, breaking your glasses was always a great way of skipping school, sadly at an expense to my parents, but it did get me wondering about eyes.

Two strange but beautiful holes in your face but, but I had this bearing important question, if I was to look at something in front of me, let's say a few feet away, where was I truly seeing the object, was it a few feet away or was I seeing it in my head? Looking at it closer, like a blood hound on a scent, I recognised that light was going through my eyes – lenses in to my body for processing.

So, the big question was, where was I seeing the world and the unquestionable fact was .... I was seeing everything from the inside, everything was happening within my own self, like the projector in the cinema ....

To change the movie, I realised I didn't have to change what was on the screen I'd have to change the information on the projector and....... this got me thinking.

Yes, your happiness is happening within you;

Sound, silence, light, darkness, joy and misery are all happening within you. If someone touches your hand, you may think that's coming from the outside but these sensations which people are feeling are coming from the inside. When we grasp this concept, people may realise that nothing external can affect them without their permission as you are, the keeper of your own projector.

As a child, I first realised what mortality was when a young friend of ours died in an accident. Before that, I thought we were all immortal as active kids, climbing, swimming in the rivers, crashing bicycles and go carts, overcoming sickness and so on. We seemed to frequently escaped death all the time, but .... however, this death of a friend where one minute he was here and the next he had vanished had a profound effect and made me wonder.

When I looked around, why do people take life for granted when tomorrow is promised to none of us? You can trust me on one thing, you'll not be here for ever. One day you'll pass this life like all the others before you and whatever you believe to be your status or position in life will not save you or me either.

So, from that point onward, when I woke up in the morning, I was now aware that others didn't wake up, particularly my friend........his time had passed, so I realised I must not take life for granted.......his passing had helped me wake up to my own mortality.

So, IF ....yes, I deliberately put a capital IF –you and I wake up tomorrow, surely this is a fantastic thing? Over a million people will not wake up but I did.

I always look around and smile, I'm still here and a million people who were precious to someone didn't wake up. So....... check those five or six people who are precious to you and make sure they all woke up too.

Well WOW it's a fantastic day already. You woke up and everyone that matters to you is also here too, that should be enough.

But isn't the problem people are living with the idea that they are immortal. They're not conscious or awake to their mortality.

If you're not conscious of your mortality, then somehow you must think that you are immortal. Does that make sense? How many moments in a day are people conscious that you are mortal? If you were truly conscious, would you have time to complain about stuff? Would you have time to fight with someone? Would you waste time doing some rubbish stuff with your life?

This one thing, if it was taken 100% seriously each day, would be life changing.

~3~

Aware

N ow that I was becoming more aware that there were signs and new learning opportunities happening all around me, I just observed everything in as many ways as possible some. I'd try to make some sense of it without attaching myself to the events. I had a deep feeling that all creation or the conscious system wants us all to succeed.

Like a good guardian guiding children to develop and grow, it wants you to grow, even in the most difficult situations. I quickly felt and realised that the point of our being here was to make choices and if creation can help along the way, it will when it's to our own benefit and in the right direction.

It realises you are engaged, but not always aware because sometimes the dramas in people's lives distract them from learning. Sometimes people just need a little nudge, a little help, to become unstuck in life. Let's call it a little push in the right direction from time to time.

Other people can do well in certain areas, but not as well in others. You may be caring for others in one way, cooperative and even when you look in the mirror you may see yourself from a certain angle, but other parts need to be worked on. We all know someone who can be the kindest person in the world but then has an anger management problem and tends to fly off the handle a lot, then get upset and later apologise, maybe repeating this behaviour over and over like a broken record. So now comes the nudge to help overcome this, it could be subtle or a shock. Sometimes you are the tool for someone else's learning along their journey; you are part of a plan to help them to learn too. Some groups of people work very well together in their lives bringing out the best to help each other. At times these people are in different countries, but eventually they all need to come together with each other to interact in little projects, so this is where that little nudge comes in again. You may get a feeling like, wouldn't you really love to move to Australia, I will use Australia as an example as I have family there, you just get this strange feeling that Australia is a great place for you, you don't know why, but you just get that sense that you always wanted to go there. Maybe creation won't make you go, as you have your freewill, but you may need to go to meet someone to help you with your growth there. You may think it was circumstance having this urge to travel to this country and another circumstance that this person was in such a situation in that exact same time and so on, but it was for you, so this was not just circumstance; it was a chain of events for you and that other party to come together.

So, become aware of these little nudges and ask yourself on a daily basis when you recognise a chain of events happening, a phone call, a text, a video online, a commercial, it can be endless possibilities, eventually you will become sensitive and be ready to act and flow with them. Go with the flow, my mother use to say, and she was right. Sometimes the nudge will be for you and other times you will feel it's for someone else but giving and receiving are the same things to the evolved being.

In the small village I lived where everyone knew everyone else and their business, people had their likes and dislikes, sometimes you come across a cranky neighbour whose mission in life is just to annoy people!! Of course, there can be many sides to this comment but, as a child growing up, you may only see them as bad or wicked. I always thought that deep down there had to be more to them than that, as they really were only like older children and were not that different really. Was I simply making assumptions about them?

But what are these assumptions that humanity uses on such a huge scale? Is there any truth/value in making assumptions at all, is making assumptions hallucinatory in one's own imagination?

Isn't making assumption's, someone generating something that doesn't exist? Doesn't this just sound insane? But for many this is their norm. Someone has assumed something to be true and now the mind is running away with itself, it's just imagination out of control. I concluded that the sadness and drama in one's life can be directly rooted in or connected to making assumptions. Isn't there a battle happening between humans making assumptions and taking things personally and attaching themselves to it? So, if we remove assumptions from our lives doesn't that give us clarity which removes the content of imagination and the drama of it all? When we add gossiping to the making of assumptions, now we have a cocktail of poison and this can become an epidemic in society. However, isn't this just an epidemic only because some people hadn't the courage to ask for clarification to get to know the truth and instead just made an assumption based on no foundation whatsoever?

The good news is that we can change this very simply by just acknowledging how many times in one day we make assumptions about anything and everything, ideas flooding in your mind! When you are listening to people, become aware and acknowledge when they are making assumptions. So, now that you have this new awareness, trust me you will see it a lot.

Police all assumptions as they arise but don't act. Take control and say NO, this allows people to take control of their lives. Just become a witness to what is happening, you will start to remove some of this drama in your life for good, and live in the truth of life and not in a state of hallucination.

My Mum mentioned once that this neighbour was only unpleasant because she was unhappy with herself. At that time, I couldn't understand the choices people were making.... was it a choice, or was it all in the mind and people couldn't control themselves? or maybe they liked this state, or was mental commentary the culprit. Isn't this all about the ego attaching itself to feelings of frustration, anger and resentment which encourages one to complain or argue all the time? If you can't tell what is causing your frustration and your unhappiness, ask yourself, is it the situation? Or are people unhappy because of what their mind is telling them about what's going on? Isn't this happening to millions of people around the planet?

A large part of people's unhappiness is not caused by the situations around them, or the conditions or even people. The greater part of their unhappiness is caused by a mental commentary about the situations that people find themselves in, confusing their own mental chit chat for the true reality.

Here is a ridiculous example. Let's imagine you're queuing up at the supermarket and you start to feel irritated, with an aware state of mind you might pose the question, why am I unhappy right now?

Well your answer might be, I'm unhappy because I don't want to be standing here and having to wait for so long. I'm unhappy because the cashier is so slow. I'm unhappy because I don't want to have to do my shopping after a day's work.

OK, you get the point, so really what has happened here – the mind has started a one to one conversation with the self....... but really all you're doing is standing in a supermarket in a vertical position looking around and breathing - that's the true reality.... when you dismiss this commentary, life is simpler.

Look at all this overthinking people, how they influence people's moods, states of mind, decisions and so on. All this is happening from a negative perspective because the ego loves the drama. Unhappiness is made in the mind and once you realise this, you gradually relinquish the unnecessary self-debasing chit chat in your daily life. Become a witness to reality and let go all unnecessary mental commentary about what's going on around you. There will then be a total shift in your life's experience.

However, changing can be difficult, when you tell yourself you don't want to think certain thoughts, that is precisely the first thing your mind will produce.

Let's have an experiment, I will ask you now NOT to think of balloons- red balloons, big red balloons, try harder and yes, you think of balloons. You see, you have to first think about something to try to not think about it; it's a paradox I know but this is just the nature of your mind. If you want to change thought patterns, you can exchange the thought process rather than trying to forget it.

I'll give you an example; a young man came to me with regard to a traumatic event that had happened to him. He was surfing in the sea, got into trouble in the water and nearly drowned. In the coming weeks following the event, he experienced flashbacks of it and physically he avoided water as it triggered those flashbacks. All this was creating PTS, post-traumatic stress syndrome. He was advised by other people to forget about it and move on, but isn't that the most ridiculous statement and advice to be given? As I have explained above, every time he tried his hardest to forget the event, the memory of it would become even more powerful.

To exchange the thought pattern is the opposite of trying to avoid the thoughts. It means to bring it up in the mind and to change all of the events in the memory. The young man agreed to try anything.

He had enjoyed both surfing and his lifestyle so, by asking him to close his eyes, we began with him talking about the events of that day he experienced trouble in the water. Now he was in the water, but we started to change the event; the water was made of chocolate, lemonade, flowers - it was his choice. Yes, it sounds ridiculous I know.... but stay with me. The surf board was made of a lollipop stick and it had a tree growing out of it in many colours with a little family of miniature people living in one part of it and cartoon characters on surfboards surfing beside him. The full moon was its brightest with the stars lighting up the sky behind him OK....... you get the picture? It sounds foolish, but we're only playing with the imagination of the event and the psychic traumatic energy attached to the memory of the real event. By repeatedly replacing the memory with fun and laughter, a new memory was formed that had no stress or anxiety energy attached to it. The memory was altered into a ridiculously fun event and the emotion attached subsided simply by exchanging a thought pattern rather than attempting to forget it. This tool can be used to exchange all thought patterns from the smallest to the most serious, the choice is yours.

Being told to trust your gut feelings seemed to be the answer to all unanswered questions while growing up. I didn't like gut feelings as my gut feelings were changing all the time, nor did I always trust them, but I was open to giving them a chance as perhaps the best and most beautiful things in the world cannot be seen or even touched. I learned later in life this would offer a great sense of awareness but it is a feeling and not in the mind. If you have a gut feeling about something, follow it. Sometimes gut feelings can be danger signals and sometimes they're welcoming signs for people. Either way, your body seems to be a capsule, just one way for your higher self to communicate with you. There can be many outcomes so one must be patient. Look back at your past decisions. Did you trust your gut feelings? Did they all work out? Were your gut feelings confused because of your ego, previous beliefs or fears or the powerful imagination? Sensitivity is required to heed these signals, don't try to second-guess or override them with logic. We all have a higher self and this higher self that created everything is at work in great harmony and thus can see the greater picture. You don't have to challenge your higher self.

You may be thinking, what happens when you go against your intuitive wisdom, well you may have feelings of unhappiness, sadness or anger for some reason or maybe feel resentful, frustrated or guilty which acts as a trigger or makes you feel as though you are swimming against the tide and therefore everything seems to become difficult. Always go with the gut feelings that feel good and always come easy to you because that's the sign that you're on the correct path. Heed well the signs that feel uncomfortable or are difficult for you. This will heighten your intuition. In time, you will be able to differentiate between the imagination, trusting your gut and guided feelings.

~4~

Neighbour

Those of whom we surround ourselves in life is so important. As an adult having a neighbour who always seemed to have an answer to challenging questions good or bad was great to keep you thinking, either way I was lucky to have one.

I didn't hesitate to ask my many unanswered questions. I once asked this neighbour about human behaviour and without hesitation, she provided the answer.

She said" some people are just wired wrong" .... we both laughed as she had a great sense of humour, but I knew at that moment this quick answer. I had been given a little nugget of information and maybe there was great depth to this answer.

Is it possible that people are wired wrong I questioned later by myself? If we break it down to the beginning of one's life, we have to ask are we as people born suffering from anything? If your answer is no, then all suffering that person may have experienced since birth has to be entirely self-created along one's way.

It makes good sense to me that it has to have accumulated over a period of time. For a high percentage of people, it is psychological suffering,

So, what is psychological suffering? It's simply negative feelings arising in the mind relating to the mental and emotional state of a person. Again as no one else is in control of people's minds, this is choice people are making. This means every human being has the choice to suffer or not to suffer. We make choices every day; we choose the clothes to wear, the food we eat, the friends we hang out with. You can use your imagination or thoughts to think in every possible way.

First of all, again we must start by taking full responsibility for our lives and destiny and accept that these are in our own hands. Yes, I have heard a thousand excuses over the years why someone can do this and can't do that, but this is all psychological drama. Have you come into this world to experience life or just think about life? I mentioned this many times and it always went unnoticed – talking is not doing, most people have a cognitive bias, meaning that many people seek information that only agrees with their previously held beliefs. This can be very dangerous as it does not allow new ideas or possibilities to manifest themselves in order to help their growth. This leads to poor decision making or the recycling of old information from the past that already hasn't worked, nevertheless almost like a Mantra, they continue to repeat the old patterns and hinders growth as there is no change.

If you want to change your suffering, you can start with a physical action. Many years ago, I walked the Camino de Santiago for charity, which is trek across northern Spain. Making this decision to become involved in this action became a life changing experience for me because I became more intently aware of myself and the life all around me. My view of life changed and any psychological suffering I may have experienced beforehand was truly being replaced by new thoughts and beliefs. We could call this a rewiring whereby previous beliefs fell by the wayside, just by this one action of walking for a number of weeks carrying all I needed in life in one rucksack. I quickly realised everything I needed was with me, I had enough and I was enough. This has become a metaphor for my life so I remind myself every day that everything I am carrying also in my personal psychological bag - my beliefs, the heaviness in my heart - are things that I have accumulated over a period of time, these are my choices and nobody else's, therefore this is my personal bag to resolve.

It is hard to always create pleasantness in your life with home, family, work, etc. For many, we are looking for everyone to cooperate with us, to be on the same page in a sense. Does this ever happen? Can it happen? No one ever cooperates one hundred percent. Have you found even one person in your life who does - your husband, your wife, your partner, your children, friends or neighbours? I have a grumpy old cat who doesn't cooperate 100% either. Even she does her own thing....

But internally, within yourself, you must have 100% control, there is no wiggle room here. People's biological instincts are very strong, survival and procreation are very powerful and, if we don't take control, these instincts will take over. So, we must look inside NOT outside for full control. I'm not a gambling man but I reckon your odds are much greater because, with the external life, there are too many variables happening all the time. However, your internal life is all yours to control. You can be the dictator of your own being if you so choose and it always makes me laugh that so many people choose to look in the wrong direction. If you control this 100%, you will get 100% pleasantness in life and, if you choose to ignore doing this, you are losing out on a great possibility.

Our instincts are very strong and powerful and we have this innate yearning for relationships. I have a friend at this moment who is using technology to try to find a partner. He is willing to travel to Peru to meet a girl he has been talking to online for six months. That instinct to form a relationship is so strong that people would travel halfway around the world in the blink of an eye.

If we are honest, are most relationships made for the sake of convenience, comfort and wellbeing? This statement probably won't make me popular but are most relationships simply a mutual benefit scheme deep down? Do most people just have their own self-interests at heart? Its sounds harsh I know, because we have this belief of romance picked up from movies and books about finding this other half, this other part of our self. Isn't it just two opposites making an attempt to become more inclusive? Most people may not be consciously aware that the life within you right now is longing to break free from boundaries and to be untethered and has no interest in being tied down to anything. You want to be free.

Some people use relationships to try to convince themselves of this self-similarity or oneness......we both like ice-cream, the same TV shows, to dance, do yoga, share zodiac signs etc, etc. Where sexual pleasure is involved, this drives two people towards each other with the innate instinct of the desire to procreate. Sexual pleasure can be a liberating action for people; it is a creative space for one's expression and is very powerful as it offers moments of boundless freedom. Most of us can live quite a structured life, working for 50 years.

People must get to grips and understand that you can never become one with someone else which sounds very obvious since, at the end of the day, you are two single entities. People must learn to enjoy the opposite. You can also be lovers and enemies at the same time and that's OK too if it's what you want, but you must enjoy your unique individual self not depending on another. If we constantly look for someone else to help us to feel happy then once more, we are looking in the wrong direction because the feeling of love is just a feeling that has opened up inside of you. It doesn't need to be created by a situation, it was always there and, like a flower, has just lain dormant waiting for you to awaken it.

The next question is usually asked, how to move to become love? Is something that has been philosophised for an eternity? People often wonder what they have to do to change themselves to become the greatest part of their human existence, which is love. I came to the conclusion that fear lies at the heart of this question because fear produces ego and ego is a supporting partner to fear. They are the Bonnie and Clyde of interference. But there may be a part of ourselves that likes this drama being played as a distraction, instead of dealing with the challenges involved in change.

Fearful people like to question other people, they only see the world in a position that they are at the centre of, a centre of their own universe and they only see everything in a relationship to themselves. They judge other people based on how well they match up to them. Do you know anyone like this? Fear creates beliefs because, if you have uncertainty, uncertainty makes most people nervous, they like to know what is going on so the drama begins.

When we don't have certainty, which is almost all the time, we come up with beliefs and those beliefs make us feel good, feel better and/or more secure. The problem with a 100% held belief is that you become rigid in that position. This is a trap where you become selective, based on whatever your beliefs are, so fear creates this ego and these beliefs. Fear can be very covert, a slippery fish that is sometimes hard to see.

If I was to ask any individual to tell me what their fears were, most people would probably list one or two or they might say that they don't have any at all. Remember, fears can be very subtle inside a person. It's the same with beliefs. If people were asked what their beliefs are, I would also get maybe one or two suggestions

One's culture can play a big part in this and, if you were born in another culture, your beliefs would be different.

Ego is very easy to spot so, if you want to change yourself, start with ego any time you feel negative, anxious, upset, angry, agitated, annoyed and so on, basically any negative feelings about something. That's ego. If you didn't have the ego, you wouldn't feel negative at all. Most people go through life feeling a whole lot of more negative things than they do positive things because people are mostly programmed and run by fear but, to complicate things further, fear is also a protective human trait for survival.

When you feel something negative, just identify it and trace it back to its origin and ask yourself where did that negative feeling come from? Why is it like that? When things happen, ask yourself why did I get angry about a given situation? Always remember you choose to be angry, it's not that someone made you angry. You are making choices all the time; you can be angry or not be angry.

When you've identified your own fear, you must then own that fear and here is where the real honesty comes in. Let's say you have a deep-rooted fear of being inadequate and when someone uses this against you, it pushes your buttons and you start defending yourself to try to cover that up. First you must own it and say to yourself, I really don't want to be that way and ask yourself why you should have this feeling? Remind yourself/become aware, "This fear is not helpful, it's not even true.

To move to love, we must identify anger and defensiveness as it rises in the body, just say the truth to yourself, this is not who I am. Take a position of power. Tell yourself, I'm not going to feel that way and transform this moment by saying something positive rather than saying something negative from feelings of hurt. Eventually, as you repeat this process over and over again, that fear will start to dissipate. You'll find these fears and that ego will have no foundation at all and now you can start to transform to love.

~5~

Cleansing

Growing up in a sporting family was both good and bad. When you question life, you need time to think a lot, but the structure and routine required to become good at a sport wasn't always on my radar at that time. I had bad eyesight and was as blind as a bat without my glasses.... but conforming to the norm like my siblings was to be applauded so, please excuse the pun, I played the game. I could not escape questioning everything even playing sports, I found that every contact made with the outside world, everything that we touch, seemed to leave a memory in our body. If I asked you to close your eyes and I put a ball in your hands, you would recognise this ball without your eyes seeing it. Likewise, if I handed you some money, you would quickly realise it was a piece of paper or a coin or a stone because, after the body has touched something, it holds it as a memory not only in the mind but also in the body, So, everything you touch in a single day is also creating memory and that can be a lot of stimulus which can leave the physical body out of balance, not at ease and perhaps at times confused since it can be the source of too much stimulation.

Do you ever feel cleansed, revitalised after you've had a shower or a bath? While travelling through India as an adult, I noticed people in India would put their hands together to greet people *"Namaste"* - no touching another person, no shaking hands like in Europe or hugging like when I was travelling in Brazil. It was explained to me in

India that they were aware of this contact and the memory held in the body for thousands of years, showering once or twice a day is a way of washing off all contact with the external world, they call this a water wash, a quick dip in the sea or a slow flowing stream also works, as does an air wash in windy weather when one would stand front/ back facing for a total of thirty minutes with eyes closed and being conscious of this. Of course, a good shower is good for hygiene to preserve health but it also can to balance and harmonise one's self and without balance and harmony change will be slow or none at all.

~6~

Who am I?

My first year in secondary school I deliberately positioned myself on the blind side of the teacher. The teacher asked everyone to introduce themselves and while I was trying to blend in with the paintwork like the invisible man, she asked me the ultimate question, "who are you?"

I explained my name, my hobbies, my family but it didn't seem to satisfy her because she picked holes in each of my answers. At that same moment there was a fire drill and I knew it was a sign and that I had been saved from utter humiliation. But I had this burning question? was I just a name or a hobby or part of a family? I had to answer this question so I asked a few friends but this soon turned into a comedy sketch so I knew I had to look deeper or find some friends with more dept......so I broke it down back to the start, maybe I was a grown baby and, whilst that maybe true, a little further input was required......So I came to the happy conclusion that the body is just an accumulation of food. Our mind is simply an accumulation of impressions gathered through the five senses. The traditionally recognised methods of perceptions or senses - taste, sight, touch, smell and sound. What you accumulate can be yours in a sense but it never can be you, for isn't it just storage and a function of memory in the body and mind? Are we more than just body? Like entering a maze, the deeper you go in, the more questions seem to come up. Then I came across this word called consciousness, and this consciousness was within us all. We all have a feeling of who we are, we are not what we identify ourselves with in any physical manner. Sadly, most people try to live their life through what they have gathered in life, rather than identifying who they truly are. In moments of near-death experiences, all these illusions disappear and you're left with your true self and it is only your true self that matters.

Like a bad penny, this question would repeatedly come up in conversations over drinks and at college. I knew as it had come up once more, it remained unresolved and I once again had to enter the maze of information to try to make sense of something that 99% of the people around me were really guessing. I started from the opposite side this time, firstly acknowledging what I wasn't. I wasn't anything external, using logic I taught how can something that comes from outside of you be you? As a golden rule here, we must rule out anything you think you are, because that is just accumulation of impressions in the mind that you have just attached yourself to it - jobs, relationships, family, all sorts of stuff, these are simply things that you have picked up along the way. However, if we question this more deeply, 'Who AM I' which is beyond all thoughts and is not coming from the outside then it becomes clearer. I really like the way it is explained in the teaching of the legendary sage, Sri Nisargadatta Maharaj, which can be divided into two parts.

This is getting deep so brace yourself, it's going to be a rocky ride for a moment, just let it sink in or maybe come back to it at a later stage when you are ready for this new information.

The first part is the non-verbal state. The I AM is a state without using any thought, memory, emotion, associations, perceptions, attention or intentions. So, if you cannot stay in the non-verbal state, just hold on to the I AM state and discard everything else. Here is a list of the very valuable principles from Sri Nisargadatta Maharaj:

1: There is only one substance – meaning the universe and that everything is made from one   substance

2: Everything you know came from the outside so discard this as it is not you

3: Question everything - do not hold on to a belief of anything

4: To find out who you are, you must first find out who you are not

5: In order to let go of something, you must first find out what it is

6: The experiencer is contained in the experience itself

7: Anything you think you are, you are not

8: Hold on to the I AM - let go of everything else

9: Anything you know about you cannot be

I suppose we could not leave this up in the air without mentioning the four actions happening right now in this moment - physical, mind-mental, emotions and energy - which happen every moment of people's life, yes even while sleeping too. Most people just take these for granted until they are taken away from them. Now, here's a question, since you woke up this morning what percentage of these actions are you conscious or aware of? Are you mindlessly moving through life completely unaware of these actions or are you 100% aware? By being mindful of these processes going on, people will start to become more life sensitive and will start to see others also going through life with mindless actions. To state the obvious, there is a huge amount of life happening all around you. But how many actions are you aware of? First, start with yourself and then look at others, then all life and creation - birds, bees, flowers, the wind, the sun, stars, leaves, different shapes, different colours, sounds, silence.

Look intently at light and darkness, some of the finer movements in life can be less obvious. Watch a feather float to the floor, start asking yourself the question how is this possible, what forces are at bay to aid this action and so on? Question everything, yes modern science can put a name on it, but they don't know how it truly works or what actions are at play.

With practice, you can reach a situation where, once where you observed or maybe saw very little, to a place viewing the magnificence of infinite actions. It can be hard to change, yes for me too and it takes work. I have to move out of my comfort zone on a regular basis because that comfort zone stagnates growth. It's just the brain, is a record of the past that we are recycling all the time, whilst recycling of goods is good for the planet, it isn't for growth in this instance. As soon as we start a memory, each memory is connected to an emotion and emotions are the end product of past experiences. So, the moment that people recall their memories or a problem, all of a sudden, they will feel unhappy or sad or feel pain and this demonstrates that how you think and how you feel creates your state of being.

Are you still with me? A person may be in the present but if they keep recycling their familiar past then that past becomes a projection of the future.

Do you believe your thoughts have something to do with your destiny? Yes, of course, so if you are not thinking of what you want to become in the future, you are really still projecting your past into your future and you may find yourself reliving your past over and over again and again, Similar to the movie Groundhog Day...... and wondering why life is so boring, mundane and doesn't change.

Let me ask you another question for you to answer to see if you are reliving the past? Do you always sleep on the same side of your bed? Do you get out of bed the same side? Look at all the patterns that you repeat each and every day that are similar to the previous day? year? decade? How different does one day look to the next? Are you repeating your own past, expecting a different future? Ask yourself honestly how can repeating the past change your future?

Now let's look at a child whose parents have promised to take him to the funfair the next day. This is new to the child so he wakes up excited, anticipating something new happening and the possibilities of adventure, this brings the child to a place of looking forward and exhilaration. This can work for all of us too. A quote from Sydney J. Harris – *"History repeats itself, but in such cunning disguise that we never detect the resemblance until the damage is done."*

You can change the future but first you've got to want to. Let's not just brush over this, one's true intention must first be set in place for any change to happen. We all want more but it can be challenging, I get that too. You see, every human life is in a perpetual state of insufficiency, are you aware of this? Remember, if you are disagreeing without reading this further then that's just the ego creating drama. We all have a feeling inside us that we want more and even when we have more, it's like a never-ending thirst. I'm not talking here about material things, food or basic needs. I'm talking about a psychological thirst for something that is missing inside of us all. It doesn't matter who you are, or what you have achieved. You still want a little more than you have right now. Just pause for a second and think back on your own life. Have you ever been 100% satisfied with everything?

Even look back at the great emperors of the past. Despite ruling half the world, they always wanted more, if you gave them the whole earth, they would want the stars... speaking of stars, even modern-day Hollywood stars, who seem like they have it all and we have them up there on a pedestal, feel the need for more. Sadly, however, they can be the most broken because they come to realise, even after reaching the top of their profession, they still have a psychological emptiness, some part of them is always looking for more. This is the human desire but the fundamental desire within every human being is for a boundless expansion of our inner self, definitely not the accumulation of anything external. Why is this? It's because for a while these external things make us happy which creates a memory of happiness for a moment but then they soon fade. This desire is within all of us for something more. Sadly, some people simply set a new goal of accumulation not realising that it is inwards, not outwards, that offers the answer. All human experience is 100% self-created. When you're alone and you're miserable, who are you to blame? You're just in bad company with yourself right.... It's all very funny but true, only by looking within ourselves can we remove this feeling of insufficiency.

I've been asked many times; can our thoughts have the power to influence our reality? The answer is yes, there are three ways you can influence your reality and hopefully this will come across as common sense but it is worth revisiting just in case. One way is by your interpretation of the information you receive whereby your interpretation becomes your reality. That's why people who tend to be negative see a lot of negative things because they interpret this information more negatively and why people who are more positive see more positive things because that's their interpretation. You have either option to choose, it's all about your interpretation of everything.

The second way is the way you act and interact with other people. Some people interact with people in a very negative way, let's say people just use others, there idea of a friendship is what they can get out of another person, how can I use them for my own benefit? Well, if you feel that way about people it will change the way people react to you, people will soon become aware of your ways, everyone will soon know what your intentions are, so your own interactions alter your reality.

Number three, you can modify your future with your intention.

No, you can't force the world to give you whatever you think about, but you do have an equal influence in, if it benefits your growth. That influence can be weak in people because in order to have a strong influence, most people cannot operate from anything but the intellectual level. People must operate from the being level or the consciousness level but the intent must be for the betterment of not only their own evolvement but that of others also. Sadly, most people are conditioned to operate from their intellectual level based on logic or past experiences. They are not working from their authentic real self. For many, like a character in a play, they are playing a role or fitting in, we even dress the part to own this role - I am a nurse, I am a police officer, a priest. This is not their true self. If people keep thinking from the intellect, with all this mind chatter drama and play-acting going on all the time, people will not have a good solid meditative state and they cannot let all the other thoughts go. You may still modify future probability with your intent, but it will only be marginally. People who can calm their mind of thoughts, maybe using the Wim Hof method, meditation, chanting, yoga, exercise, it could even be fishing, to name a few. They can use this intent to project their future probabilities; they have a lot more power to manifest their intent as it is based on a foundation of growth and openness to change and for the betterment of all. Here is the catch though, once more it must be from an inclusiveness way not only for oneself.

At this point you may be saying, oh gosh, I don't fit into any of this, I am different, and I agree you are different, all of us are totally unique. The information in this book can fit into your uniqueness and your freedom. The first step toward to personal freedom is awareness.

Your whole life is awareness; awareness is what you are. This is the very basis of all life. You only know you are alive because you are aware of it. If all awareness disappears on this level, we can call it death.

First, we must be aware that we are not free in order to be free. I know it sounds silly but to solve a problem, we need to be aware of the problem - maybe this sounds more logical? Awareness is not always something that you do, actually the less your activity inside is - the more present you are without all the personality, identity, life's dramas. For some, this is 24/7, seven days a week, 52 weeks a year, just relentless dramas. These activities are happening at an unconscious level but we are the ones who are undertaking enormous activities to maintain all of these, when that activity is lowered, one's awareness becomes heightened. These traits have not disappeared, you can still be as crazy as ever, but they have lost their impact on people, they don't mould people anymore.

Awareness is the deepest dimension of the mind and connects you to the very basis of creation. When you get in touch with this state of heightened awareness, yes sleep is just a different level of awareness. Suppose you're dozing off and someone shakes you awake. Boom the whole world comes back to your awareness in a single moment. You recreated the whole existence instantly. Not in seven days but instantly, in the blink of an eye. Awareness is a process of inclusiveness, a way of embracing your entire existence. If you keep your body in balance with thought, emotion and your energy properly aligned, awareness will bloom for you. If you go through life just eating, sleeping, procreating, reproducing you are just like any other animals in the world but as a human being, you have been given awareness. This is a great gift but sadly 90% of the population are unaware of its full potential because they are not life sensitive, they are simply going through the motions of life. When you are consciously in touch with your awareness, you gain access to the subtlest dimensions of your physicality in life and this must become the new norm.

When I was growing up, I was in a family full of likes and dislikes. The family might be described as dysfunctional as it didn't fit in - here's that word again – the norm. But what family has no form of Dysfunction?

I never identified it as such and I didn't take any position at all. When I say position, I don't mean I went all quiet or dumb when things had to be said like others might have, or conform to the certain hierarchy structures that were already moulded in this one house, supporting certain members of the family that complied with this structure while isolating other members that didn't comply. This is because it doesn't matter what your likes or dislikes are in life, these are all different types of bondages and distortions. At this time, I thought everyone knew this, but sadly not. Both types of bondages distort the perceptions and the balanced view of any given situation. When a position is taken, that view becomes altered. If something is liked or disliked, people will exaggerate this in their mind. Have you noticed this? People speak kindly about one person and harsh about another, to exaggerate something in people's minds means you cannot see them for who or what they are. To resolve this; question do we cure other people or do we cure ourselves? If you are hungry do you eat or do you give the food to someone else to fill your own stomach? If you are sick, do you give your medication to someone else? Of course, not.... so as soon as you can see yourself in others, it will become much easier to connect with them. With this perception and connection, you and I will discover the unity of consciousness and inclusiveness which will help to remove the bondages in life and lead to one's upmost clarity.

We are all here to transform, that is why you are reading this book and why I spent so much time putting it together. For any transformation, we must first identify what is blocking this transformation. There are three big blockages and traps here - fear, beliefs and ego. First, we must identify each of these. Ask yourself what are fears, beliefs and this ego that are much talked about. Right now, if there is a voice in your mind answering, no I don't have them, we all have them in abundance it's just people are just not aware of the signs or maybe are in denial. This is a big subject so without boring you, I'll just scratch the surface.

When we identify what these three are then we must learn to let them go and remove the blockages or entanglement that involves us with them. If you are successful at identifying and removing these, a transformation in this lifetime will be successful, everything will become much easier and you will return to the natural state of who you are.

Holding on to fear is mostly about holding on to untruths. Yes, if there is a wild animal in front of you and you think you'll be attacked that is another story.

Yes, do feel fearful but I'm talking about social fears, a fear of death, a fear of living life to the full, a fear of being foolish, being wrong, fear of what other people might say, think or do, a fear of sharing, love and on and on.

We've got to let all that fear go as it cripples growth, plus they are all untruths. You don't have to be a prisoner as most of time this is just a feeling and/or imagined. You feel fear by using imagination to create something that has not yet happened.

The belief system can be as simple as cultural, religious, family or an identity one is holding on to but it leaves little or no room to expand because any new information may not conform to the already held belief system and therefore growth is halted and the belief systems rule out all other possibilities. Expansion is at the core of transformation so your beliefs become your limitation.

Ego is just another product of fear and beliefs which all fit together as snug as fish in a sardine can. In fact, so snug it sometimes goes unnoticed so, if you get rid of the fear, usually the ego goes too. Instead of seeing things the way they are, the ego sees most subjects negatively and the ego wants you to see things this way. Once again, no room to manoeuvre with the ego. You see things that satisfy only the image of you and of your reality, it is one directional and the ego is constantly getting in the way of you seeing the truth. You become pigeonholed.

The best place to start a transformation is to clearly and honestly ask the questions - how do I find my fears, beliefs and ego? Then how do I work on them to let them go and not continue to fall for these constant triggers/traps? Yes, these are a big part of your genetic code for self-preservation and are very strong instincts which are great for self-protection in the wilderness but you are not in the wild so they can be toned down to suit your urban environment. This will lead to a transformation.

Most of us are compulsive in our behaviour. A high percentage of people suffer from one form of compulsive behaviour or another, so people are in total denial about their compulsions or fail to recognise them. In modern day life, there's compulsive shopping, hoarding, eating, gambling, drinking, sex, dating, exercise and even gardening. I could go on forever. These behaviours don't necessarily lead to an end pleasure or reward, but the compulsive person engages in the behaviour anyway.

When a person has a compulsion, they are trapped in a pattern or repetition and it involves senseless thinking in that they have created a pattern of thinking for themselves and these behaviours can prove difficult to overcome.

Yes, you may see a pattern forming here, but first we must recognise that this compulsiveness is happening. So, why are people compulsive? Is it simply that they are unhappy with their current situation, they have created a new pattern of thinking for themselves and have a hunger for more life? Look at your own life, how many times a day do you feel a compulsion for a certain act.

Take, for example, overeating, you know your stomach is full but you have this internal feeling that you want to abstain from self-control, you want to be free. This freedom is just another dimension in you that wants to throw away the shackles that restrict you and for you to become boundless, to expand ...... freedom!

This dimension is a feeling, but people try to replace this feeling with materialism, these actions can become compulsions. People can't replace freedom and/or being boundless with materialism or physical actions.

This dimension we want to touch is within us all – it doesn't come from an external source. There is a higher dimension of nature within us and that is what we are yearning for. This dimension can eat up all information and continue to look for more, this hunger will raise you to a higher state of consciousness, but we must identify and remove the shackles and bondages of compulsions and transform these compulsions into a higher dimension of the true self.

~7~

Growing up in a small village

Growing up in a small village, it was evident from an early age that self-preservation was the key ingredient, get a job, build a house, have children, conform and let time do the rest. To be successful meant having money, a fancy car, anything materialistic.

I bought in to this business model of success too.

When I was a young man and came across the internet for the first time.... There weren't many computers in Ireland at that time. I believed this virtual world would eventually house virtual shops on it, which is now commonly known as a website. I taught I could now make my fortune by providing this business and service. I felt this could be a huge opportunity if I could get it started early as technology was changing very quickly.

To start up I needed money to gain specialised skills in this area and this came at a huge cost. So, I approached my bank who laughed at my business plan. Determined not to give up and being young and foolish, I eventually I got some none salubrious loans and found myself in trouble even before I could start and I was brought to court.

Eventually the judge threw the case out calling it a storm in a tea cup as he could see the loans were almost payed back and I had never been in trouble before, he also laughed at my business model saying I was ahead of my time and the local newspapers loved this heading. I knew my working career or any future business ideas were finished. I was now the talk of the town with many people feasting on my situation. Sometimes I would meet a neighbour or some friends I had grown up with would cross the street to avoid looking me in the eyes. I had so many knives in my back at that time it was unreal but, instead of feeling overwhelmed, there was part of me that felt liberated in a sense. I had now experienced the true behaviour of weak and rigid minded people. As an outcast, I didn't have to conform in any way to their way of thinking.

All I had to do was deal with those people's ignorance. I got to have a front row seat to see how my friends and family reacted, they all took the predictable route, all silent except my mother but she always was fearless and had her own mind to think for herself and never treated me any differently. I respected this courageous stance very much because it's so easy to be weak and conform to the pack. It was all very amusing really. ..... but this one event triggered my interest in human behaviour and without this chain of events I would not have studied psychology at a later stage, there would be no books written.

By now my Mum was living in England, we spoke most days on the phone.

She was very intelligent about life but crazy in other ways. She had lots of analogies about life which I soaked up like a sponge and would constantly laugh at.... She'd say the phrase, *"I wonder why"* in a humorous manner during most conversations and it seemed to fit most situations... She mentioned one day, *"What's on your path will never pass you"* which got me wondering about life paths and especially mine at that point.

I was later to find this quote from Krishna while doing some charity work in India,

"It's better to do your own path imperfectly than to do someone else's path perfectly"

I always wanted to go to India as it seemed to be the spiritual hub of the planet but I had one problem, a fear of flying, I say a fear but more of an anxious flyer, although at that point I had flown many times, doing short haul flights around Europe which I deemed bearable and a necessity.

One day I said enough, I needed to go, it felt right. On checking the internet, the flights were too cheap to pass up. I could feel a chain of events happening so without hesitation I bought the tickets to leave a few weeks later. Upon arrival at the airport, I was randomly upgraded to first class which, for me, was another sign and I knew everything would be OK.

While I was travelling through India, I questioned these paths and I was told by a Guru there that we all have a path in life, at the moment of conception a path for your physical life is created by your higher self. He mentioned to me have you noticed that something's come easier to you than others? Or have you ever felt you have reached a point in your life where you feel you have nowhere to turn?

Not to worry, for worrying alone creates a blockage and only through a clear mind can your own true path be revealed to you. First, be conscious and surrender to the fact that the answer will be shown. This means you must detach from the outcome and let it go. This sounds a little ironic but just trust that it will come to you and, all in good time, it will, but patience is needed here.

You see, your life is about touching everything. I mean by touching everything, to use your life to experience anything and everything you can and, yes, I mean everything. Try different types of jobs, dancing, gardening, ride a motorcycle, go hiking, play music, be creative, whatever comes to mind, don't just talk about it, physically do it. By trying everything, whatever you get involved in becomes a part of your own experience. Have you noticed, on a physical level, yourself getting sick a lot? It seems as though you're constantly unlucky or unhappy, annoyed or frustrated? This Guru told me that there can be physical signs to help awaken people, to rouse you and divert you back to your original path. Staying with the quote I started with – *"It's better to do your own path imperfectly than to do someone else's perfectly"* – seems very fitting here.

The next question usually is;

How do we recognise our path and/or what's meant for you on your path? This is easy even if people don't have the sensitivity to feel which direction to go in, when you try lots of things. They all become part of your experience. I mentioned already it's the one that brings you the most joy and the one that comes easy to you, that is your path! Any action you have to labour over and over and over again is not for you, you may believe something is on your path, a specific job, hobby, or you may like to emulate some other person. If you have to try and try and its all just hard work, maybe frustrating, stop immediately. This is not your path. If it was your path, it would come easier to you. Yes, it could be challenging to gain a level of skill in anything but this skill should also feel inspiring to you and doesn't feel like work, it's challenging but a joy at the same time.

Many people go through life choosing the wrong path, justifying it because of money, basic needs or logic, doesn't this sound insane to you? Your life will be over soon enough, no two people have the same finger prints, so why would people think we should have same identical similar paths?

You are 100% unique, there's no one like you, period! My question to you is ……. do you want to go through life labouring each and every day or do you want to float through life waking up with blissful enthusiasm on your true path that comes effortlessly? Whatever level of success you've achieved already can equally be achieved on your true path without the labouring.

The vital instrument for change is detachment. The problem though is becoming intertwined in everything we touch, people just become stuck to it. When people get stuck, they have no manoeuvrable space. Why is this happening? It's because people's involvement in everything is selective or discriminative. You might find this statement a little harsh but look at all the likes and dislikes people have in their lives. I like this, I don't like that - race, culture, the weather, food, exercise, sport, TV, social media, basically everything.

For today, try it yourself. Start by looking at the people around you. Some you'll know, others maybe not, just see if you can you look at every person you meet with the same sense of involvement without being selective or discriminative in any way. Yes, for instance, use social media too and scroll down through profiles without any taughts going through your mind such as, I like this person or I dislike that and so on.

Now look at the air that you breathe, the land you walk on, the animals around you .... remove all the likes and dislikes of everything around you. If you can manage this, there will be no room to get stuck to anything. Your life will not be selective or discriminative, there will be more balance. Your life is to experience everything without becoming attached or and/stuck to it. This is detachment.

You may have a direction in life, however, it's best you have flexibility to flow and change. Your intention is very powerful, you can direct this intention to this oneness of the universe for help to change your position also, whatever it may be. At the same time, you must also be detached from the outcome too. I have used this more than once in my life and it has proved to be a very powerful technique as long as your intentions are to become more inclusive to everyone and everything. That's the key here, you can't ask for things involving only your own personal gain alone because you can't be separated from the oneness of everything and everyone else.

Like being part of the ocean already mentioned, you are floating and bobbing along with everyone and everything else, you can't be separated. Our living experience and the whole universe works in perfect, inclusive, harmony.

~8~

Resentment

I've seen a lot of resentment in my life both with regard to family and in social situations .... people taking sides and positions, sibling rivalry etc. I thank them all for those experiences as they have defined who I am now and it has clarified to me, how fearful people are. As my mum often said, "time is a great healer" and again she was right. Resentment and anger are all self-defeating. You can't have a harmonious relationship with anyone and at the same time hold onto resentment for them. And you definitely cannot hold onto anger and bitterness and still have a healthy heart and a settled stomach. Medical studies have proven that holding on to anger and resentment is clearly damaging to our physical and emotional health and well-being.

The energy of resentment eats away at our minds and bodies. You may have noticed this when it's seen etched on the faces of bitter and angry people in society. Maybe there was a bitter teacher in school when you were a child growing up, perhaps a bitter friend or family member always complaining about life and other people, one minute playing the victim card the next they are manipulating their position to get their own way? You can see their eyes narrowing and their lips tightening.

Forgiveness is the only way to heal all wounds. When I was a young man, I worked at the petrol pumps serving petrol. Even then, I looked for spiritual signs, my antenna was up all the time.

I realised any situation can be a metaphor for great learning no matter how monotonous the tasks seemed at the time. I came to understand a connection between forgiveness and serving fuel to customer's cars. In life we need forgiveness to become unstuck from situations to move on. I noticed that, each time I lifted the fuel pump lever, the number gauge on the petrol pumps would reset in much the same way that forgiveness works. When we truly forgive, we reset the dial like on the petrol pumps and then that part of life is reset and we can move on.

Always a great place to start is by forgiving your parents, brothers and sisters, friends and so on. Yes, I'm sure there could be a long list depending on the network of people who have shared people's life, forgive them all, then ask for forgiveness too as it is equal and it goes both ways. This is a very powerful tool. Although it sounds very simple, don't discard it. Make it part of your everyday life. Sometimes we're wrong about things, sometimes we have made assumptions about something or taken a position on something else. It happens; with me too so many times I can't even remember. I apologised to everyone at one point but I also seen that can go unnoticed to the receiver but that's ok also. I took responsibility for all my actions so as not to hold on to anything heavy in my heart. Ask yourself why it is so hard to ask another equal human being for forgiveness?

Is it because asking for forgiveness removes one's power? Has the ego got that much power over people?

Moving from fear to forgiveness - are we afraid of what response we will get? Or are we afraid that we'll have to confront our true selves? Asking for forgiveness for all the things you have done to others resolves this unconscious psychic energy that people are holding on to. All of this is just holding people back from moving forward but your intention must be pure otherwise you are only fooling yourself because, again, you may be able to hide from others but you cannot hide from your own self and this is your own singular journey!

When you forgive all creation for anything/everything that happened or is happening in your life, you finally forgive yourself. Once you forgive yourself, the self-rejection in your mind is over and true self-acceptance begins.

The source of creation that created life seems very logical to me now as I write this, it seems to want us all to optimise growth at every turn and it will put people into situations when they are ready for the challenge to grow. A position which is just enough to grow from but not too challenging that they are more likely to fail .... like a good parent who allows their child to fall once in a while to help the child to learn, to grow more aware and to become independent. So, creation seems to try to pick situations that you, the being is ready for, something you can build on.

Of course, I'm not talking about material success here, I'm talking about emotional growth, evolving, character building, something you can grow from which lays a healthy foundation to evolve from fear into love.

If you are given too much responsibility so that you are more likely to fail or regress rather than succeed, it doesn't make sense that the system tries to put you there. It's best you always go into a specific setting where you are given the choice to continually evolve. This means you could be born rich or poor restrictive or open, just about what you need in order for you to grow, but you seem to be free to make choices at all stages, an example, you can take something that is very challenging and do well at it or be miserable at it, people have the choice.

We all know people that are able to flip any situation to the betterment of themselves in the most difficult of situations. We also know others who seem to have it all but yet can make a misery out of everything. You're not guaranteed a win, you're just guaranteed a good set of challenges and choices that you have the capabilities to handle to evolve and grow if you choose.

When we talk about creation, people talk about a God in heaven or a God of everything overlooking everything else but really, we are talking about the source of our own creation.

Basically, I am talking about from what or where we have come from, the source of our being. You and I may be quite different in our human experiences, but the source of our creation cannot be different, that's undisputable. The important question is, have you experienced the source of your own existence yet? Or better still, is it possible that people could be existing here without understanding the fundamentals of who they are?

If a person has realised that they are living here without understanding the true fundamentals of whom they are, this should be a huge thing, the pain of not knowing should be so huge it should be an overbearing question. If people go through life not knowing who you are, this realisation may not have sunk into people awareness yet, isn't it the fundamentals of all life to know one's self and where we came from? Firstly, to really be aware of this question you must understand the pain of not knowing. This is the start of awareness and then you can't be here without knowing. This higher state of awareness means you have to know, every minute of the day you're wondering. Like an orphan seeking their biological parents, once the burning in people is so strong, people are on the correct path and all the accessories in life - jobs, money, relationships, your basic needs - will all seem superficial to this one desire to know one's true self. With this new found awareness you must learn to think and dream the impossible; many people are a slave to their conditioned habits. To break free from this conditioning, it's only through repeated thought that the impossible can become the possible. Like all repeated actions, for example driving a car or learning to dance for the first time, it may seem impossible at first, but by repeating the process, the mind readjusts to the tasks and normalises the process. It removes the disbelief and it becomes a newly instilled belief. So, if you want to break out of the mundane, think the impossible and make it possible then think again.

In a very little time and through new achievements, a belief in a world of endless possibilities will surface and you will start to realise the brilliance of yourself and of life.

Everything you've done in your life so far has been in pursuit of one single thing, whether you sought a career, started a business, made money or built a family or just sat around for a while dreaming, it was always because you wanted just one simple thing, JOY.

Let's take a look at some domestic animals. I have a cat so I'll mention her for this analogy. The moment her tummy is full she's completely peaceful.

For a human being, hunger is one problem but for a human being with a full stomach, there are still a hundred problems. Why are we so different? Aren't we part of the animal kingdom too? Survival instincts are a huge issue in every life, but for human beings, life doesn't seem to be satisfied with only survival. Human life only begins with survival! We are looking for JOY, when you are naturally joyful you are naturally pleasant to the world around you. If the level of joy is declining, it is as though people are gradually committing suicide via slow death. If you're not joyful in yourself and you're looking for joy from an external source you're looking in the wrong place. When you have a greater awareness of existence, you'll be in a natural state of joy in whatever you do. Unfortunately for most they are in a state of, "I don't like this, I don't that". These are all forms of dramas with the mind out of control.

I want you to imagine a world without fear, prejudices, anger, greed or hate and imagine a world in a joyful state. Again, we will start by imagining your family being joyful, you got it? Now your extended family being joyful. Still feels good? Excellent, now your community and so on until you have covered the earth and universe that we all share. How does the world look to you? We are all searching for joy. Regrettably, a high percentage of people are not even aware of it. In India, the greeting "*Namaste*" is one of the most beautiful of greetings - the divine in me bows to the divine in you. I see you, beyond your strengths and weaknesses, beyond your achievements and your hurts, beyond your personality. I see the pure light that you are. Imagine if everyone practiced only that one greeting with true intent and meaning every time when in the company of another? Everything starts with ourselves, when we project joy to everyone and everything that surrounds us, it becomes infectious and it costs nothing. One intention, just try it until it becomes a natural state for you. You will immediately feel more joy, energise yourself and see people responding with the same intention to you as this transaction of giving and receiving becomes one.

But be warned you may find as soon as you try this the ego is put in an unfortunate position. Yes, everything around you are nice for a while, you may find that the ego will come up with some negative mental commentary because it's always searching for unhappiness, like searching for food or water to drink. To liberate yourself from the ego, don't tolerate the negative mental chit chat. Yes, recognise it but realise the trap that's happening, it's like knowing how a magic trick works and after that you will never fall for it again. You don't have to come to any conclusions or form any judgments, just recognise it and let it go. Become empowered and start to rise above negative thinking and stay in the presence of emptiness and calmness and of course, distraction can be also a useful tool. My Mum liked to say, "God loves a trier"........ from an early age, I thought I should try everything at least once, as crazy as this sounded it would lead me to many new positions and directions in life.

When I came across the ancient technique of chanting (mantra) on my travels, I had to give this a go. For thousands of years chanting has been practiced by many cultures in many countries for spiritual and/or health reasons. It connects us in a very real way to the furthest reaches of the higher dimensions in us all. Whenever I mentioned chanting, I always got strange looks and smirks forming on people's faces like I was insane...... The fact that the whole universe is ignited by sound waves is undeniable. Chanting your own sound waves is used to heal and ignite the higher self in people and science too has now proven that chanting can help to induce the relaxation response. This response is defined as the individual's ability to prompt their bodies to release chemicals and brain signals that cause muscles to relax, respiration to slow down, blood pressure to drop .... all from simply chanting.

Different sounds have different effects on the human psyche. We know the soft sound of wind rustling through the leaves soothes our nerves, the musical notes of a running stream enchant our hearts, thunder brings awe and fear and we all realise that musical sounds affect us emotionally. A solo child singing in a choir can create such beauty in us. By daily practice, twice a day, morning and evening, a few minutes of chanting can create a balance of people's physical body and mind and a pleasant distraction from the ego. When we calm the body and mind the real shift in dimension elevates and our physical health and wellbeing can and does dramatically change.

"Our health is our wealth" .... this proverb has been tossed around for millennia but I feel, although people say these words, they mostly take their health for granted.

There are two types of ailments, infectious and chronic. Infectious ailments are caused by an external source or an invasion coming from outside the body. Chronic ailments are those that last more than three months and are created by peoples own body's cells attacking that person from the inside instead of protecting them. I feel 70% of the ailments suffered on the entire planet are self-created because they happen within the body. What happens within you can and should be fixed by you, does that make any sense? It therefore follows, what happens from outside of you, needs outside help. If you suffer from chronic ailments, ask yourself a quick question. Why would your body work against you? Why would your cells attack you when their true purpose is to protect you? Is it then plausible to say that our cells are more intelligent than we know and are trying to tell us something? Science has proven that living cells change in different environments, they've memory and carry information.

Are our cells trying to tell us something? Encouraging us to create a different environment for our higher good? Why is it, when people change their direction or path in life, they can experience an immediate recovery from an illness or stop getting sick? Why can cells switch on and switch off on different occasions? We see this with the placebo effect, people are not being tricked, they are just able to switch off the ailment or disease themselves. How can one person abuse their body through alcohol and drugs, smoking and over eating the worse diet and still live to 101 without their cells attacking them whereas a non-smoker, non-drinker gets cancer at the age of 40?

Let's use an analogy, if your cells were your close family, why would your family or in this case your cells turn against you? Therefore, it can only happen when they're not happy how you're living your life?

I've had many deep discussions regarding this subject and came to the conclusion that the cells' that make up our body's want to create growth and harmony. When someone has a deep passion for something, for instance, painting, dancing or anything which comes quite naturally that gave them tremendous joy as a child .... as an adult because of the pressures and constraints of simply living and paying bills, when that person ignores this passion the results can be disastrous emotionally and physically. Again, life is about choices where people choose to discard their passions in life and end up working in a job they totally dislike, eight hours a day, five days a week, year in year out. Yes, the money is good, but they feel deflated going to work and when they get home have no motivation to do anything else and become bitter, angry at life, they are celebrating Fridays and dreading Monday's mornings. Some may turn to alcohol, drugs, food or anything for escapism or avoidance, creating new patterns of behaviour and disruptive cycles. Even without this happening, their cells may start to create an illness so as to avoid going to the work environment they loathe. It's a scientific fact that the stress we create for ourselves regulates our genes and creates disease with long term effects. Let's look at all chronic pain for example. If you're of a certain age you may know someone with cancer or arthritis, maybe MS, I know many. Ask yourself how many do you know that were born with these ailments? The genius of being a human means we can turn on stress responses simply by our thoughts alone. Thinking about our problems immediately turns on those chemicals and our daily activities can trigger them and make us sick

The flip side to this is ...... if our thoughts can make us sick, our thoughts should also be able to make us well. Does this sound logical to you?

Let's look at the emotional reactions people have in their lives. Let's take an event, something so shocking that you can clearly recall it in detail, the brain focuses all its attention on the cause of this event and then creates a snapshot of the event in the mind, we call this a memory. Long term memories are created by highly emotional experiences so what happens then is .... when we have an emotional reaction to something, we think that we can't control these reactions. Well, it turns out that if you allow that emotional reaction to last for hours or days, we call it a mood and we've all had one of those. We say to someone "Hey what's up with you?" and people when honest might reply, "I'm in a mood".

If you could tease out that mood with them, they would say it was because of something that happened to them, say five days earlier. They are therefore holding onto one long emotional reaction to an event and have relived it over and over again for days.

If you keep that same emotional reaction going for weeks or months, we may call it a temperament. You might ask the question again, why is he or she so bitter and angry all the time? Once more you may get a similar answer ...... this thing happened to them nine months ago or even back as far back as a child. A person can keep that emotional state going for years and then we call it a personality trait.

Learning to control the onset of an emotional reaction is of vital importance. What's really happening is, the mind is unconsciously calling something an "event" because the survival hormones are directing it to pay attention to what happened so as to be prepared if it happens again. The problem is that most people spend up to 70% of their life living in this survival mode and feeling stress because they're constantly anticipating and living out the worst-case scenario based on a past experience. They're emotionally embracing this experience with their beliefs and fears over and over again and again. Yes, even when they're in bed or supposed to be enjoying a pleasant walk in the park, they're creating this on-going stress for themselves. Some people may be smiling now as you know you've been that soldier. This is a very serious subject as it is very detrimental to health. In this moment, people are in no danger but they are still reliving a state of stress and fear and this conditions their body into a constant state of fear.

When people do this long enough, the body's stress hormones down regulate the genes and can create disease with long term effects just by these thoughts alone. This means from the time of becoming attached to it they self-created an internal believe and unable to change that state of mind since it happened. Now the body doesn't know the difference between the actual event and the recalling of it. Their thoughts are directly causing continuous stress on the genes in the body. Please let this sink in for one moment, a person can be seriously affecting the formulation of their cells that preserve health.

I hear you ask, "How can we reverse this? Well it's quite simply .... bring yourself to a state of balance .... acknowledge the event, become detached from it and make light of it and truly feel forgiveness. When we change the psychic energy of the memory, it will dissolve and dissipate.

Evolution and fixing ourselves is the growing process. We're all evolving based on how we act, perceive and believe. Then we use this information for the next life choices, big or small that we have to deal with. This experience then gets recycled back as the input action for each lesson learned and thus the next lesson becomes easier. The more you experience, the easier it is to learn more, but if you choose ignorance, it will be difficult to even get started. Fear of change and ignorance will go a long way in blocking any natural growth.

However, every time you make a choice in the right direction, the next good choice is an easier choice. If a child of nine years asks an adult, how do I grow up? There really is nothing you can tell them other than explain .... Go through life making the best choices you can.

When we make good choices, we grow up much more functional than when we make bad choices. Everything about growing up is a process of life choices, not a set of rules like driving a car, because life is changing all the time, it doesn't maintain a rigid structure.

The best and most important thing we can do to contribute to all life is to fix (heal) ourselves. When you heal yourself, you'll always want to help and pull up others. Giving others a hand up is a sign that you are evolving.

In my life I've experienced a lot of coincidences. I was aware of these at an early age as my mother was quite spiritual and would mention in a humorous way, that coincidences were signs not to be dismissed. I felt deep down she knew more than she was letting us know. For me, coincidences are messages from the infinite intelligence of life. I feel there is a higher intelligence within us all. I call this waking up to the clues from creation, urging us to break out of our conditioning. We all regularly experienced coincidences but how many of us really notice or react to these signs?

Our thinking patterns can block us from moving forward and sometimes we need a little help, like the road to Damascus moments, where we see clarity for a moment and it changes our life direction. For many, this can be like switching on a light. For a moment, think of all the coincidences you've had in your life .... even simple things like thinking about a person, then getting a call from them or when you keep meeting one person in many situations. You may pass all this off but this is a moment to become more attentive, even more alert to a message for you or maybe it's the moment to offer some advice or kind words to help someone else. Many years ago, I was searching for some computer software and came across a programme that allowed people to use the internet with your voice. It featured voice recognition which was fairly cutting edge for the time. I was very impressed with the way technology had progressed and I thought this could be such a useful tool for someone. A few days later, I was in the company of a small group of friends when I was introduced to a man who had lost his sight only nine months earlier. He mentioned technology could help him a lot and straight away I told him about this software. I immediately recognised the coincidence happening. The next day I installed the software on his computer. His life became more interesting and enriched. I live in a small town but have never met that man since. People may create some rational reason for this scenario but just look at the chain of events that happened to bring two strangers to meet and you realise it's very possible that this was a guided coincidence for us both. Each and every one of us have an inner awareness to play an inclusive role in all life.

I've been very lucky to have a good friend with whom I shared many travels and trips over the years. When I met him first, he mentioned he was a qualified chef. At the time I was quite impressed but was later to find out that he was the worst chef on the planet. His brother and I often laughed about the mashed potatoes he made from a packet of Smash consisting of milk and powder. He was always very generous at making and giving food in his home and indeed was the designated food provider. When

I mention vegetables or salads, there was always a running joke - in his quick wit, there was always a one liner ready to be released like a prize fighter. We had many discussions about food and at one point, when his brother was very sick with cancer, I tried many times to make the connection between food and our physiology and health, explaining as humans we really are an accumulation of food.

For example, we eat a piece of food and within a few hours the human programme converts that food into human body. A horse eats the same food and the horse's programme converts that food into a horse and so on. We've established that we have a human programme and other animals, mammals', insects and so on have their own programmes also going on. Hence what we consume is very important. What we consume becomes part of our cells, bones, tissues, organs, etc. Internal organs are built from the nourishment that we provide our body with through the foods we eat, this is all common sense.

We are what we eat is true. Our nervous system is also continually altered by the consumption of certain foods. Again, this will not make me popular but it must be noted all caffeine products – tea, coffee, alcohol, drugs, garlic, chillies, onion's - all affect our central nervous system. They give us highs and lows like the peaks and valleys when walking over a mountain range. They stimulate our body into altered states. Yes, some of these stimulants are good when people are ill as they're medicines but they should not be consumed in times of good health.

Healthy foods are full of life and should not be taken for granted as foods can alter our thinking. Healthy foods are foods grown from the earth which are nourished by the sun, water, air and the five natural elements. Cooking depletes the nutritional value of foods but does allow the body to digest them more quickly so we must find a balance between both cooked food and fresh fruits, nuts, salads and seeds. The value of seeds is tremendous because they represent the concentrated life of everything on the planet. Nuts are nature's way of showing us that good things come in small packages. These bite-sized nutritional powerhouses are packed with heart-healthy fats, protein, vitamins and minerals to create great balance in the body.

If you feel you have to eat meat, this is my theory – this should be done only on rare occasions because you're eating meat with cells and these cells have an emotion and a memory coded in them equal to human cells. This is why raw meat (Mayo clinic) can take up to thirty-three hours for men and forty-seven hours for women to digest and pass through the human system. All meats create excessive bacterial activity in the body which can make the body lethargic and puts added pressure on the digestive system.

We hear a lot of talk about protein - protein this and protein that, but only 3% of the body is composed of protein and excess protein can cause harm to the body. Carbohydrates are a major food source and a key form of energy. We need carbohydrates for health and energy but they must be the right kind of carbohydrate, completely unprocessed. For clarity of the mind, we must also be mindful of what we consume as what we consume has a direct effect on our health, our moods, how we think and feel. Below the age of thirty, three meals a day is enough to sustain good health. Over thirty years, two meals a day is enough because the metabolism is slowing down. Obviously, there may be some variants depending on one's lifestyle. Our body and brain work best when the stomach is empty. I know we all love food and this may be an unpopular subject so let's look at it this way. After two and a half hours, food starts to move out of the stomach and you have more energy, agility and alertness as the body is not in the process of dissolving food.

~9~

Children

Having children becomes a real game changer for many - for most representing a change from selfishness, I need this, I need that to selflessness where now the roles are reversed. This is usually the time when children realise the sacrifice of their own parents.

The question is do we really own children? They just come through us. Yes, I do know about the birds and the bees but this book is about stretching the mind not just recycling what people already know. I'm talking from a universal point of view.

We are all just part of the ocean of the Universe. I feel one life does not belong to another life. That life has chosen to be with us, so cherish this and value it. For instance, the troubled teenage years I hear people complain about all the time, aren't the teenagers really trying to tell you that you don't own them? That independence has become their best friend. You should see them as an equal in life. Yes, it's most important to give them responsibilities in the home you share, in the decisions you make, encourage problem solving minds, have full involvement with them and this will nourish and enrich the teenager's mind about all the possibilities. Isn't the problem, we keep trying to fix everything for others and not allow each person to fix themselves?

While growing up, I saw a lot of anger expressed and I didn't have to go too far from my own family to see these outbursts. Anger is the quickest expression of pain in the body. The technique we'll talk about could be applied to procrastination, compulsive behaviour or any actions.

Let's stay with anger as an example as it is so destructive. When you're very alert, you may catch the anger rising in yourself, you know what I mean. We've all felt that rumbling in ourselves like a volcano about to blow its top. You may not be able to stop it at times but when you feel it rising that means you're aware of it and you can choose either to watch or stop it. The energy is still there but it can be like trying to stop flowing water in a stream. When you don't witness this event, it's going straight into your mind, you are 100% involved. When you can't catch it ask yourself at what point were you not conscious of it happening? This all depends on the degree of one's present awareness, then look at your justifications or reasons for allowing this to happen!

Ask yourself this fundamental question, why is my mind out of my control? Why am I deeply unhappy about this particular moment or situation? If you look closely, you'll see that this situation is actually only a little thing.

So how does it trigger such huge pain in you? Let's say someone doesn't answer your phone call, you might feel reasonable about this the first few times it happens but if it continues and you keep calling and still get no response and feel ignored, all sorts of deep-rooted pain may become triggered within you. Maybe as a child you not acknowledged. The stored memory of that pain is still felt in the body and is rising.

To another person who doesn't have a trigger connecting to this inner pain, this insignificant situation means absolutely nothing and they've no understanding of it and may think, you're crazy. Most people hold some form of pain in their body, dormant waiting and observing and for some they may not even know it's there. Let me give you an example, which I'll call the sleeping cat syndrome. As I have an old cat, I'm prone to using cat analogies. For those who have cats you may notice they sleep a lot. However, when you look carefully you may notice a sleeping cat is not always fully asleep. They know what's going on. From the slightest noise to the unfamiliar they're always scanning and are totally aware. You could be cleaning up, showering, getting dressed, closing doors, still no movement from the cat but all of a sudden if there's a tiny rustling sound like a mouse, boom the cat is fully alert and up.

The inner pain in the body is like a dormant cat. Whilst being very sensitive to the surroundings, all kinds of things can happen which do or don't trigger it but it's there, silently waiting for a situation, an event or someone's remarks during a conversation .... then they are fully alert with an outburst like, "are you accusing me of something, are you saying I'm a liar, are you calling me fat, do you think I'm stupid?" and so on. So, the cat is fully awake. Generally, we hold this suffering in the body but the body uses the mind to express itself.

To counteract this, when you see it in others or yourself, apply complete stillness. I learnt this from a friend and I felt it was right. As you listen or feel the emotion rising, the ego mind will try to draw you into becoming part of the story, the old story is brewing which can be a trap .... as soon as you fight with that person or yourself, you become part of the story. Yes, you committed yourself, you made a decision and you have a choice. You can say this person said this and that person said that, or I feel this or that. The truth is, as soon as you start talking, you activate the exchange. If it's coming from the outside, that's their doing, not yours. If it is rising in you, you still have choices either way. You can say to yourself silently, I'm not going to play this game and become a witness to this event and not take part in it. This way you choose to stay in a state of still presence. Is it easy? Well yes and no, it all depends how connected to, in control and/or aware you are of your own inner body. Whilst you're listening, stay grounded be deeper than the surface drama and keep your mind still. It's much easier for you to connect and/or disconnect with that person when your mind is still and doing nothing.

Avoid connecting with the story. When your stillness connects with their inner being and your inner being, you're separated from the story so the drama dissolves quickly.

We must become consciously aware of our own deep-rooted pain. Surrendering and acknowledging it with honest forgiveness will start to dissolve the pain and outburst of anger. Fear is always the silent intruder. It traps in such a subtle way from the inside which over a period of time can slowly strangle until the day comes that there's nothing left.

We all remember people we grew up with. They were light-hearted, witty, maybe playful but over the years became bitter and uncomfortable to be around, this could be friends or close family. When around such people, I call this 'on time', meaning I'm extra alert in this situation. Think back to your younger years. Were you fearful or fearless? Did you notice a change happening? Can you remember ever being carefree? People's fear is 100% self-created as it starts from inside. It's a form of imagination and when repeated, it becomes a part of us.

Have you noticed we self-sabotage our dreams and ambitions all too quickly? We convince ourselves to give up just when our dreams are within reach. Does this sound like sensible behaviour? To have a vision and want a dream took fearlessness and imagination so why are you/we so determined to stop it happening? Our biology is trying to protect us at all times. Fear stops us from taking that step out of our comfort zone into the unknown. But isn't fear just in the mind? Aren't most people living in the mind instead of the true here and now? When fear is always about what is going to happen next, that means fear is about something that does not exist - does that sound logical? When fear is about the non-existent, fear is one hundred 100% imaginary. Could that be true? If you're suffering physically and/or emotionally from something that doesn't exist, don't we call that insanity?

I once visited a mental hospital in a local town called Enniscorthy in Ireland and although it may have sounded like a very obvious question to ask, I asked the nurse, what do you think is the problem with most of the people here? She replied without hesitation, "their imagination has run away with itself; they're imagining things that are not happening". This wasn't the most technical or scientific answer but don't we see this happening all the time in society. Many people socially accept certain levels of insanity because the large groups of people are social proof it must be right. If someone is suffering from anything that doesn't exist, this must amount to 100% insanity. When people are suffering in the present from something that happened years ago this is suffering something that's past, it no longer exists in the present.

The problem is that people are rooted in their own minds. The mind is one-part memory and another part imagination. Both of them are, in some way, a form of imagination. People become lost in their imagination and don't stay present and that's the basis of fear. When you're rooted in your present reality there is no fear from the past. Honestly ask yourself on a moment by moment basis, what's actually affecting you right now, this minute?

If there's nothing affecting you in this moment let's move on to the next moment and ask the same question. Continue this awareness throughout the day and wake up again tomorrow and repeat this process until it becomes the norm. This is living in the present time, not in the imagination of your mind, not affected by the future or the past. This will aid in removing fear from your present existence.

However, we must be flexible at all times as a flexible mind is not one for drawing conclusions. There's a way to live your life without taking any positions at all. Looking at life with every possibility and in every possible direction is a good place to start and avoid getting tied up with anything or to any position. When you take a position, you become stuck in one direction. A flexible mind doesn't take a position. Truthfully, we really know nothing in the great scheme of life, this planet or the universe. We have given names to things that make us sound very intellectual but what do we really know? We really don't know how our planet spins in space or even what space is. We have no idea of the solar system. We don't know when we'll die or where we go when we die. Even how a blade of grass holds the memory of how to reproduce itself or a flower, I could go on forever. When we constantly look at everything fresh from no position, we're less likely to miss out on endless possibilities. Where others see nothing, you will see all kinds of things. Where others see problems, you'll see possibilities because your mind has the flexibility .... staying flexible is the major tool here.

I was 17 when I left home for the first time, moved to another country with all the feelings of fear and excitement, the great unexpected but also the powerful feeling of independence. This really had a transformative effect. All the safeguards and training wheels were well and truly off. Living in another country your identity now comes into play as you become labelled based on how people identify you. I hadn't thought too much about this thing called 'identity' as I felt it was another trap that humans made up to discriminate. Once your intellect is identified with something you lose your true perspective on life. Ideas good/bad, right/wrong, body, gender, family, race, creed, community, nation, qualifications they're all mental constructs. What was considered to be moral a hundred years ago is intolerable today. What I thought as good, my children despise. Have you noticed this? You also disagreed with your parents' and grandparents' ideologies; I know I did. The moment you become identified with your limited ideas you're looking at it completely wrong and you have become rigid in your view.

Your intellect becomes moulded around these identifications in such a way that you never see the world as it is or the wood from the trees so to speak.

If you chain yourself to your identification you may feel comfort or feel safe in this group and of course the ego will provide you with 100% support but you become imprisoned to your own limited group of ideas and beliefs - all your thoughts and emotions will spring from that identity and/or that camp of ideas. When you identify yourself as belonging to a chosen profession, all your thoughts and emotions flow from this identification. When you identify yourself with your nationality or religion, they also flow from that source too. It's endless, what people have identified themselves as ...... career, materialism, money, music, sports, sexuality, parenting, hobbies, the list is endless. People attach and identify themselves to many things, we must lose this attachment as, regretfully, the intellect functions around these and they can represent and influence a certain level of prejudice to everything else. If humanity learnt to drop those identification's and realised, they don't have to identify themselves with anything, life would be blissful.

The moment you're no longer identified with anything, that's when you become pure consciousness and/or awareness. When that consciousness or awareness surrenders to the infinite consciousness of everything you now touch super human levels of understandings of life.

At this point in 2019 it's been recognised that the universe consists of 192 elements although there'll doubtless be many more discoveries. In Kung Fu which I studied for 20 years, we dissected these down to the five elements - earth, water, fire, sun, air and space. As humans, we're made up of these five elements also and you thought you were different than everyone else! There was a time when we saw these elements as Gods and treated them with the highest respect as we realised our life totally depended on each of them for our survival. Sadly, for many this concept is long gone, taken for granted or have no awareness of them at all.

However, we can unlock the elements in ourselves. Firstly, we must understand that we're made up of these elements and also directly interconnected with every element around us. No one is an island on their own. Remember we're all just part of the universal ocean. As your awareness grows, you'll treat the five elements with devotion and respect which will lead to a new connection in your life with existential meaning.

It seems fitting to mention existentialism here as it's a philosophy centred upon the analysis of existence and of the way humans find themselves existing in the world. The notion is that humans exist first and then each individual spends a lifetime changing their essence of nature or finding the meaning of life through free will, choice and personal responsibility. And of course, we were given the gift of consciousness. The fact that humans are conscious of their mortality separates us from any other species on the planet. Making decisions and responsibility about your life is what existentialism is all about.

The big question, what is the goal of life? This question only comes up when people aren't living life to the full. When living life fully and bursting with enthusiasm this question rarely arises. The goal of life is to live totally! This doesn't mean to party every night. It means, while you are here it is best you experience all aspects of life before you die. Every aspect of life should be part of your experience. This should happen for every living human being but most people experience only 10% of life and then pass on. There's way too much emphasis on the mind and the way we think rather than experiencing life itself. Why is it so important what other people think or what you think, what people think of you or of them? What the whole world thinks of you has no existential relevance. Whatever your thoughts are right now, it has no relevance to your life, it has only psychological relevance or social relevance. Too much thinking can cloud people's existence. It's only that people haven't known life fully nor in any way other than thinking and this is not living life. It sounds very obvious but this is only thinking life. Fear is always ready to show its head when asking people to look at themselves.

People's purpose in life is to experience everything they possibly can. When you've not explored life in its magnitude but limited yourself to just the instincts of the physical body then fear is a natural consequence because your physical body's instincts are only there to keep you protected. Isn't that how the human race has multiplied with our body's self-protection and procreation instincts? There is another dimension in your body and this dimension yearns to be free.

People are limited to its life span; that is a fact. So why would anyone waste time? People are 100% responsible for everything they are and 100% responsible for everything they're not. People are the makers of their life so remove this idea of living in fear. Yes, be conscious of your basic instincts that are trying to keep you safe at all times, recognise what is happening but then make choices that feed your inner desires. Live moment by moment and continue to honestly answer this one question. Would I rather die doing something that gives me joy in life or live in a life of fear and then die? Life is too short to keep playing safe. I'll let you in to a secret, *you can't get out of life alive,* so enjoy what you do.

All choices and excuses define your life experience but learning to live a life without fear is one of the purposes of this life, to understand fear in its entirety and not fall trap to it.

An old friend mentioned a book he'd being reading. He said, "giving and receiving is the same thing". Probably to his annoyance, I did ask questions until I understood his interpretation of his statement. I had my reasons for this as I'd noticed many failings in his own life through alcohol dependency and gambling and I hoped he'd become more mindful of the importance of the information he gathered and shared. I feel all life operates through dynamic exchange and giving and receiving are different aspects of the flow of energy around us. I only have to look outside my back door and I see trees. They don't ask if you want oxygen nor do they reject the little animals or micro systems living in them. The trees just give and don't care if you want what they have to give or not. An apple tree continues to bear fruit, not concerned whether you are hungry. Millions of actions in creation are happening each moment on any given day. Nature doesn't ask or look for anything in return. It's up to the receiver, it's their choice to receive or not. Some people have the attitude that they won't give as it will not be received properly or they'll not give unless they get something in return which implies a transaction. You must forget this nonsense; this is not growth or inclusiveness.

All creation is a balance of inclusive giving and receiving. When you give and others have the sense or awareness, they will receive it. If they don't need it, or are unaware, they'll not receive it. This is not for you to decide. All you have to do is to give with a mind-set of living with the balance of inclusiveness and staying present. When you keep the joy of giving with this understanding, life will flow for you.

You'll feel more connected with all creation and more balance but always remember that to give and receive are one and we are here to serve each other.

We all have instincts. An instinct is part of the behaviour of a living organism. It's inherited, not learned, it happens naturally, without anyone even thinking about it. A hungry baby cries through instinct, ducks follow their mother by instinct. If there isn't any learning involved, then this behaviour is an instinct, I guess that would be a good way of putting it...

There are two basic forces acting within humans, survival and procreation - this is something we are aware of. When we look at it from a biological point of view, there are more organisms born than can survive on our planet. Some individuals will be more successful at finding food, mating and/or avoiding predators and will have a better ability to thrive, reproduce and pass on their DNA. So, nature has created survival and procreation instincts in human beings to survive and reproduce as a race. Most people when they have basic awareness see these survival instincts as being in conflict. One is the instinct of self-preservation which compels people to build walls around themselves to keep safe. The other is a constant desire to expand and to become boundless and free. These are not opposing forces but I feel they've been misunderstood. One forces you to root yourself well on the planet while the other takes you beyond your instincts but you can be both. Just by understanding their functions gives you the choice to avoid becoming trapped in either and thereby hindering peoples own development and expansion as a human being.

In my life I've seen a lot of anger, people angry about the most trivial of subjects. I quickly realised all this anger was rooted in a false perception. The idea that anyone can change a given situation by losing their temper and forcing their will on another - to me that's insane. The idea of trying to gain control over others in a situation is another form of lunacy. I always looked at these people with disbelief as if, for one moment, they actually were gone mad but the next minute they're normal. Does this sound like a balanced person to you?

Once again I've heard so many people making many excuses "someone made me mad". Again, this is another form of imagination or an illusionary state. Just ask the question, how can another person control you and what is in your mind? Or, reverse this for a minute, can you control other people's minds? For all your control happens from within you, not from the outside.

Medically speaking, there is scientific evidence to prove this. In a state of anger, people are literally poisoning their entire internal system. This can be verified with a simple blood test. Peoples internal system turns toxic. It involves intense activity; you may not have noticed when in a state of rage or anger that you feel completely drained after the episode. Sleep can undo the mess that's been self-created but it's all self-harming and should be avoided at all costs. When we meet people, you may notice they're holding pain in their body, they may have stories that are energised by the enormous emotion attached to this pain. This emotion is a trigger to events in one's life where there was internal trauma. We all have them in one way or another. We have to observe carefully to notice what seems to push people's buttons. The emotion is far deeper than that which being expressed on the surface so you might wonder why people are getting so upset about this or that situation. This is the human pain that lives in every human being which has been accumulated over a period of time. It's an energy field, a residue of past emotion surfacing like bad weather. You notice people becoming tense, the discontent in their eyes and often verbally outraged and/or rambling continually in defence of a specific subject.

So many people are ego sensitive, willing at any moment to defend themselves and their identity based on who they think they are but how many people are truly life sensitive?

If they walk into a forest can, they feel anything? Can people feel when it's going to rain? For most people the answer is no! People have even disconnected from the name and decided to call the forest a wood when they don't even see the trees. They've become completely disconnected. To answer this, let's look at the structure of the human body as we're made up of vibrating cells so basically, we're all a ball of energy.

Our own vibration can become stifled and compounded by other vibration around us, for instance, electricity, television, wi-fi, radio, machinery and so on, everything buzzing and vibrating. Do you think the vibration in you is able to avoid all this interference? The answer may be no, we all have a choice to switch them off. I call this 'off time'.

Our diet - what we consume also plays a big part in this. When we consume nervous stimulants like alcohol, drugs, coffee, tea, all caffeine products on top of this, they affect the central nervous system providing highs and lows in the body and often great agitation. These all lower the possibilities of experiencing life since the body is trying to stay in balance whilst all this interference is going on. I'm not saying you should be fanatical about what you consume, just consume by choice rather than through compulsion. When you do things by choice you know when to start and when to stop, you'll remain in control. If it's through compulsion when you start, you may not be able to stop. By making a few lifestyle changes, we can return and be more sensitive to life around us.

The quality of life is always decided by how you experience it, not by what life offers you. If you want any kind of transformation or new awareness in life it can only happen when you break the cycle. You can't keep repeating the past expecting different outcomes in the present. Thought and emotions are not life. Your family is not life, your work is not life, your hobbies are not life. These are just accessories to the life in you. When you truly touch life, it's an explosion inside of you. But with all these dramas and imaginations going on in the mind, these thrills in the mind become larger than life for many. When people live their lives in the virtual world rather having any physical experience at all, life is missed completely. To find life you must find something that sparkles and ignites inside of you. For me, I play music and sing which brings me great joy so I do it every day. If this is my last day, I'll leave having done things that bring out great joy in me. For others it can be something quite different, the possibilities are endless! On the other hand, if you know how to make misery out of everything that you do, you'll also have misery all your life. There again, that's their choice. Life has given humanity choices. We all have a tremendous amount of power when we remove fear from the equation. You can either live a complete life having amazing experiences whatever situation you are in or you can manufacture your own creation in your mind. So, do you want to be a living being or a thinking being? I feel that 90% of the population are only thinking about life and not living it to their full potential. Yes, I've heard all the excuses. For some, it's only when life itself is threatened they form a realisation. A near death experience or a serious illness may create a new awakening. You don't have to wait for that to happen, you have the choice to wake up and become aware and open to opportunities as they arise. (Whitney Young) *It is better to be prepared for an opportunity and not have one than to have an opportunity and not be prepared.*

When people have the notion that all their material achievements are of value only in comparison with those who don't have them, then they're trying to gain joy in themselves from another person's deprivation. Can people really call that any form of joy? Isn't this just a form of illness in the mind? The world needs to address this immediately as regretfully I see this everywhere, it is an epidemic! How many times do we allow ourselves to be totally truthful, even to ourselves, before we excuse it and allow it to continue? For one hour, become aware of all the thoughts that come into your mind. Just one hour of your life and examine what emerges. Realise what's truthful and real and what's imagination. This will help you to increase your awareness of any imbalance that may be coming up in your mind.

I'm not saying that one's imagination is a bad thing. Everything is a form of imagination at one point. For a builder to build a house, it must first be a form of imagination to begin with. We could use millions of examples but unfulfilled intentions and desires can be the source of all misery. From your imagination comes your intention and desires and they are everything. A desire is something in you that wants to be more than you already are and an intention is an expression of that desire. Bring your intention and desire into your consciousness. You can make every experience in life an interesting experience or a curse .... you have a choice and this has been noted many times. When you make misery out of everything, you've taken ownership of it ...... you, nobody else.

When you walk through life joyfully, what's the problem? In joy, everything you do is beautiful. When feeling miserable, the first place to look is in the mirror and ask yourself, what am I doing wrong? Am I thinking wrong, eating or drinking wrong, sleeping wrong, sitting wrong, breathing wrong? Most of all ask yourself, what intentions am I projecting wrong? Why am I not projecting my true intentions and desires? Why am I not taking my intentions and desires seriously? Why am I not fulfilling these? Make a list and don't hesitate. Have realistic intentions and desires, set a time period and fulfil them and reduce the misery of the unfulfilled desires and intentions that you crave, don't have these building up as misery inside of you. Take courage and resolve them. To change is, I feel, like getting on an aeroplane, etc. Yes, we can feel a little anxious, but what's the first thing the flight attendants tell you to do? Fasten your seat belt because there may be some turbulence on take-off but we all know it's only for a little while until the plane levels out and then we're truly flying ...... huge possibilities await you.

I know I go on a bit about intentions but I see this word as a mental state that represents a commitment to carry out an action or actions in the future. I truly believe in movement as it moves us away from stagnation. It's probably one of the most valuable qualities we process, change is made up from our intentions. When we focus on the intentions of others not only their actions and/or words, but by digging a little deeper, you may be surprised what you find. Being aware of people's true intentions, these can be hidden behind poor expressions. Whilst travelling I've seen this many times in rural villages and towns in many countries, where everyone knows each other. People speaking hardly opening their mouths or with barely any movement in their face or body, like a professional ventriloquist....

However, intentions can be a double-edged sword. Whilst many can be misunderstood, when one's intentions are negative and disruptive to others, we hold this within ourselves too. People may think they can escape this turbulence or troublemaking but we don't escape cruel intentions because we also create harm for ourselves. We create a chemically toxic imbalance within ourselves. That's why our mood and feelings change, we flood our entire system with our thoughts and intentions. Never forget we can't hide from our own self! Yes, you may try to trick yourself or be able to hide it away and even pretend it didn't happen. You may pretend you didn't say this or that or physically do this or that but you can't hide from yourself. It's always there in our cells. Stressed cells, yes, you've guessed it, stressed cells create chronic illnesses. You can resolve this by using your intention to be deeply regretful for your actions but again your intention must be 100% remorseful for all actions. Apologise deeply for your actions and be mindful if your intention is not 100% remorseful and genuine, you're just acting and resolving nothing. When negative intentions are repeated, they can be very dangerous as it becomes a pattern of behaviour and personality. You can see this in many people. As a child they were loving and caring, fun to be around but as they grew older, they changed their behaviour and became terrors to others and especially to themselves. It's never too late to resolve one's past with true intentions and this will, in turn, provide great growth and awareness in your life experience. Look at the people around you. Have you realised yet that they are really only looking at just another version of themselves? Or are you one of those people that think you're a separate entity? Don't you think you look the same, two hands and legs, same biology, eat sleep, breath and share equally the same challenges in life?

One of the big breakthroughs in my life was to have the courage to let go of everything. *(Someone else's opinion of you does not have to become your reality)*. This phrase should not be washed over .... does it matter where you grew up, your education, your job, what about it? There's no race, male or female, identifying with this or that, these are all more traps for humanity to fall into. We're all made of the same material that makes up our bodies. Everything is the same, we all come from the same elements that make up the world and the universe. When we die, we all decompose the same? We're mirrors for ourselves and others. We need to see ourselves in the reflection of other people. I call this the mirror of relationships. When I look around, all I see is another expression of self. Why not try this for a few days, it'll give you greater compassion towards those that come into your life and you'll immediately start to feel lighter, simply by just seeing yourself in others.

Love - In my mind I regularly hear that Beatles song ...... 'All You Need Is Love' and now you the reader may hear the song too. Love is a much-used concept but it is the path we all yearn for. Love is a feeling that happens within you. The expression 'falling in love', implies that some part of you should fall or melt away to accommodate another person. I never know why human actions should be moulded by an external source when everything is truly only happening with in one's self. It's not an action or a chain of events, love is just the way you are. People only glorify love with another because they know nothing better, it may be the most pleasant inner feeling that they've ever touched on in their life. This longing is in every person, it always remains, it never disperses. When you intensify this longing, it can become enormous suffering.

The longing we have is a yearning for freedom, to be boundless to everything. There is a part of you right now wants to be a little more than you are, to be a greater part of your existence. This is the desiring process of the body and it always wants to expand. It wants a little more, always a little more. Isn't it a fact that people only want to include someone in their lives because they themselves don't feel sufficient? ... they seek to include another person as a part of themselves, thinking that this external object will complete them and for a while, it does. However, this soon fades away.

Just imagine for a moment you're feeling complete, so complete in yourself, you're completely blissful by your own nature. If so, would you be longing to be a part of someone else? NO would be the answer. So, maybe it's time people approached this consciously and in a different way. If you believe finding a new partner in your life, getting a pay rise, buying a new house or a new car will bring you to a blissful state, you're sadly mistaken.

These are external objects and true bliss can only be created and understood from within. Love is an inner state of existence and its blissful state lies in being free and unbound to any external objects.

As a being of love, let me be very clear here, you are never anyone's door mat or have to be a pacifist. When you're a being of love, you have more personal power than almost everybody else who is a human being of fear. Look around at the people of the world who changed things, those who made massive changes, for instance, Martin Luther King, Nelson Mandela, etc. These people brought about huge changes to millions and empowered millions more. They didn't do this by force, only through love. They didn't do because they were stronger and meaner than everyone else and/or by forcing their will on people. They did it by caring, they did it with love, they did it because it was about others and they recognised this. A person of love is in a very strong position, not a weak one. It gives people the strength to help to change things, otherwise you just feed the dysfunction that fear brings out .... instead you are changing the dysfunction for the better. From this position of high personal power and awareness comes influence. People gravitate and listen to a person of love, they value what they say, people want to be near them and to emulate them, it's infectious. That's a lot of power, a lot of good influence towards an inclusive world.

This is the opposite of the person who's in a dysfunctional state, full of fear which is the weak position. Bullies are not bullying because they're so powerful, bullies are bullies because inside they are weak and fearful. They're insecure and bullying is the way they try to cover up their weakness and insecurity. To deal with a bully successfully doesn't mean you have to be bigger and stronger and match the bully physically. As a person of love, one can help the bully, not by bullying as that just emulates the bully. Always remember, a being of love doesn't mean that you're a pacifist because there will be a time when the right thing to do is to stand up and fight for the greater good, once more you're not a doormat for everyone or anyone.

Sometimes a fight can make a big change too. Although I call this a life lesson, one must get involved with the right intentions and think carefully. Again, life is about choices as these can lead to further actions ...... remind yourself of the famous saying by the brilliant Chinese military strategist Sun Tzu says, "*Choose your battles wisely*". You see, by being fearless you become love. I hope I've established that fear makes us weak. Fearlessness and love make you strong. Fearlessness could mean leaving a troubled relationship, open to new information and/or moving away from deep rooted beliefs. Moving in the direction and intention of love is our true power. This power is always within you waiting to be awakened.

Meditation can be one of the greatest tools you have. Many people are not even aware that we constantly have about 60 to 70 thousand thoughts running through our minds daily, most of which are repeating day after day, nonstop old information. In meditation, we're aiming to pause and rest these thoughts, to allow the mind to become silent and to increase our state of awareness. This may not happen overnight but then again; you didn't learn to walk immediately either. You didn't give up learning to walk after one try, we must be persistent in order to gain results, whatever the discipline may be. As Mum often said, "practice makes perfect", so practice meditation whenever you can, allow it become and be part of your life. You can practice on a train or bus going to work, while waiting for people or sitting in the park, etc. You could have a meditation space in your home. Initially you could try the Wim Hof breathing method as it will help to dissolve all the chatter your mind is so used to. We can control and restrain the mind's chatter with practice.

First, you must believe that you're in charge of your mind and that our minds do not control us. How you're identifying with everyone and everything is most important .... remove your identify from your job, family, culture, race, country, religion. I mean everything! That which we identify ourselves with creates all the chatter in our minds as you've become so intertwined with all these identities. When you remove all identities, your mind will become calm and blissful. Knowledge is an accumulation of impressions and/or information you've gathered which is only related to the physical nature of your existence. Knowing is a form of living intelligence. The spiritual process involves moving to a new level of knowing. Firstly, you must use your impressions and/or knowledge to sharpen your perception about everything around you. As they say, the finer the details, the sharper the tools.

Observe people, notice their psychological dramas and never emulate them. Recognise the worries, fears, ego, identities, beliefs and all the unconscious rambling which are not a perceptive mind. They are a mind out of control. Let's imagine a domestic animal, my cat again as an example. When I notice her franticly and repeatedly running around in circles, would you say this is a sharpened perception? No, you wouldn't! You'd see this as crazy behaviour so why is this continuously happening in people's minds? Do you think it's right to have thoughts flooding your mind, continuously running around in circles?

To sharpen your tools, first you must be a witness to life itself. I don't mean in a dream state, floating through life waiting for Friday to come as if on auto pilot repeating each day like another. Perception doesn't have to be something you do; it can be something you don't do. One's perception increases as soon as the distraction of drama and all the noise in the mind decreases .... only then true awareness of everything in life revealed.

We're all having a life experience, that's something we can all agree on. We're all seeking something else in life. We all have the hunger for more of something. What would be greater than experiencing the ultimate of life? We can seek this through our individual perception. Life is a journey toward a place where you experience the ultimate nature of all existence. To experience this, there can't be any boundaries. It has to be a borderless process because borders create limited spaces. When you calm and cease the activity in your mind and stay alert, then you're in a harmonious state of being. This harmonious state transforms the physical body from a series of compulsions of flesh, blood and hormones into a conscious process, a powerful instrument of perception and inner knowledge.

Life also means to experience the mental and physical process distinctly, not as the basis of only you but being completely inclusive of all other life and everything around you. As already mentioned, one can't distance themselves from what they are a part of. You're a part of the ocean and you can't separate yourself from the rest of the sea. When you manage to achieve conscious harmony in your body and mind in an inclusive manner then your experience of life is one 100% in your control.

To achieve this all you need to do is look inside. Creating a distance between you and everything you've accumulated from the outside sounds very obvious.

Everything you gather in life accompanies you wherever you go as everything you've gathered so far is deeply attached to you on some unconscious level. It can become stuck to you because you don't know when to pick it up and/or to put it down. It's like a sack you carry on your shoulders all the time. However, you can create a distance between you and what you've gathered and use it only when you want to but you need not identify with it!

If you can't maintain this distance, your whole vision of life will be clouded and distorted and your life experience will stay the same. Life will offer you a choice, every moment of your existence, to either become a victim or a spectator or even the very master of life. By making a conscious decision with a certain amount of daily effort and practice, we can all rewrite the software of joy and wellbeing and touch the ultimate of creation for ourselves. Now this may come across as very serious and in one sense it should. In another sense, it should be a joyous experience, for don't we see people taking life just too seriously? And if people think whatever they're doing in life is very important and serious, they need to take a break or holiday from it. A holiday doesn't mean going to

Spain for two weeks. A holiday means within twenty-four hours every day you must take a holiday from your own serious self. Seriousness has become a belief one holds onto based on one's own self-importance. Yes, yet again it is self-created. Look back at your childhood. Were you always serious? If the answer is no, doesn't that just mean one is holding themselves out to be an important person? Doesn't a successful person think the world revolves around them? Have you seen this?

Let's take a look at reality. You and I are like specks of dust in all existence. Tomorrow morning if you're not here, yes me also, a handful of people will mourn but they'll soon forget and move on with their own lives. Nature blinks and you're gone. This is the true reality. Everything in the world will continue to happen the same and move on while you or I are not here. Every human being should be aware of every single moment of their lives. It doesn't matter what the whole says about you. Presidents and leaders pass away, religious figures, scientists, philosophers, musicians, artists, all gone and those left behind move on because that's the cycle of life. It doesn't matter what work you do and/or the importance you place on it; everything will continue without you. There will always be someone to carry the baton and move with it. As you constantly remind yourself of this, you'll have no reason to be serious in life. There's a consciousness and awareness that connects all life.

As mentioned, many times, everything in life is interconnected but sadly as humans we've lost some sensitivity to this as we've evolved. We've become selective in our sensitivity but we still feel grief, feel emotion. Watching another human being hurt or abused or animals mistreated can bring up great sensitivities. For the more sensitive, they may feel great sadness to see wildlife disappear and/or nature destroyed. Even the change in seasons has its effects but many are insensitive to life's energies.

Being sensitive without being selective and to stay totally inclusive seems a lot to ask of people in the present world we live in. This means to be sensitive to the universal life energies and have a consciousness of this interconnected unity with everything. When we increase and raise our energy sensitivity and awareness a natural flow can be perceived as an inner knowing of information. A new awakening starts happening and you'll want to share this with others. When we follow this flow, new questions about everything may start arising and we become immersed in finding out who and what we are. We move into alignment with the universe and life feels increasingly fulfilled and abundantly more complete.

Your mind may be thinking money, a new house. Your body may be longing for food, water and/or sleep but your life energies are longing to break the boundaries set by your physical and mental structures to allow all possibilities to become part of your awareness. The sole aim of every individual's life energy within you is to touch the infinite, all creation, the core of our making. But first to start we must become sensitive to all life around us in order for this to begin.

The mind is a tool for exploration, not for drawing conclusions. You're born to know life from every possible direction and from every possibility. The mind must learn not to take a position on anything. When you form an opinion on something, this means you are NOT open to anything else; you become stuck to that position. Life means no conclusions. The moment you make a conclusion it brings confidence but confidence without clarity is a disaster waiting to happen. It is better to see things with clarity for, let's be honest, what do we really

know when we break it down? What are we clear about?
We trust what we see with our eyes, we may think in a
scientific way, people believe in what they understand but
how much do we understand? Naturally we have relied
on our senses, but how good are our senses?

Your eyes see a steel building? Can your eyes see
that there are holes in every piece of steel? When we put
a piece of steel under an X-ray machine, we see it is
porous. Can we think of a razor blade as having no sharp
edges? Where it really has wavy lines when we see this
razor blade under a microscope, we see that the edges are
not sharp as we believed. Still, we rely on our minds and
senses. There are lots of feelings that colour our vision.
Our mind is really highly prejudiced. What people like
they believe to be correct and what people don't like they
believe to be incorrect. The mind plays many games. In
other words, we don't see things for what they truly are.
For most, we only see them as we would like them to be.
My point is, when you look at everything afresh with no
conclusion, that is, everyone and/or everything around
you, you'll not miss a possibility. Where some see
problems, you'll see open ended solutions. Everything will
become alive to you by having drawn no conclusions
about anything.

Let's cut to the chase and look at the facts. We're in
this world, we all live in a certain country, we're in a
certain culture and civilization and we are the products of
a certain kind of education and conditioning. We've opted
for certain careers or paths, made certain decisions. I
often hear, "I wish I'd been born in another country; I
wish I had different parents, I wish I was educated in a
different way", these are a denial of people's present
reality.

We can't jump out of our skin. In a subtle way, what
is going on is that people think they know better than
source that made them. They're unable to accept the

facts of this reality They're constantly interfering with it and trying to organise this world themselves. Are they trying to have their own way? It's time to take complete ownership and acceptance of the life we've been given. You can move from the misery and madness to ownership of a powerful human mind and body only by taking ownership and acceptance of who you are. The body can become a vehicle for your spiritual growth or a barrier to it.

~10~

Physical body

Let's suppose your hand, leg or back is in pain. Now imagine this pain is severe. For most it's hard to aspire to anything higher in life because of this continuous focus on pain. Oh, my back or oh my leg, if only... The pain becomes the dominant force in your life and becomes the biggest issue in the universe. Even if God appeared before you, you would plead for your pain to be relieved first before asking any other questions. This is because the physical body has such control over us and I'm only using physical pain as one example. We are all made of life energy and like the energy of the whole universe, it can't be destroyed. It continues to manifest itself and expands equal to your part in the universe. The vessel, our human body is there to sustain and house the human existence. When life is over, it is the end of body and the body will return to the elements of earth but the life within you continues.

It's best to stay relaxed about life. Relaxation is an old concept. It means having a detached attitude and approach to life. Have you noticed that a detached and/or care free person is usually relaxed? We've all seen people that haven't a care in the world whereas attached people can be/usually tense. They can be very serious and thinking all the time in terms of me, mine, past, future, etc. They're always expecting certain results and always wanting things to move in a particular way by taking a position in certain direction. So where is the possibility of relaxation? Relaxation is a state of mind. It comes when people live in the present and live joyfully. If a person's mind remains in the past or in the future, on taking a rigid position on anything they become tense. The past is meant for learning. After that, one must let it go. Don't become attached as otherwise you remain reliving the past. For the future it best we do a little planning and projecting about who and what we want to become. Stop at that because continuously thinking and worrying about the future doesn't make sense either. A person should be prepared for everything and simply deal with what comes up, not stay in a state of tension waiting for something to happen.

There's a fine line between when people look very relaxed and are relaxed. One means being consciously mindful of staying relaxed in all situations but can be full of life and also in a state of balance. The other can be dull, stressed or lethargic. It's important to understand the difference. Anything done under stress always creates frustration which leads to further frustration. The moment we're under stress our muscles become tense and tight. Tension creates joint pains, high blood pressure, poor concentration and memory and most of all leads to poor decision making. Having a detached attitude to life and its outcomes will keep you present and in a conscious state of mind.

~11~

Mothers

One of the most positive aspects of growing up at home was my mother who, as I have said, was quite a spiritual person and this rubbed off on me very quickly. I signed up very early to this ideology. I felt it was the correct path and it came very easy to me. These two boxes were ticked and while there was great turmoil happening all around me, my inner being was very joyous and always smiling. In a way, I was detached from it all without even knowing that at the time. My Mum was very courageous as she challenged the conformity of society's beliefs and fears. In later life, she regretted some of her actions as she realised how they affected others because deep down she cared a lot. I recognised, like so many, she was using alcohol to mask the deep inner pain she was holding. At the time, I didn't have the necessary skills or words to help her .... But I feel each journey in life is a singular journey, for each individual's growth. It takes great courage for many to resist all the nonsense going on in their mind - drama, fears, ego, especially beliefs. Awareness of spirituality will come when you choose. It's not something you have to do, it's actually the opposite. All you have to do is allow the mind to be calm. Like breathing, it can be involuntary. To access it, you only need a break from all activity in your mind. While people are reading this book, my hope is that the reader does not fall into these traps in life. Like the revealing of a great magic trick, when the trick is revealed, people can choose never to be fooled again. But like all things it must be practiced to be successful, for me I reread books many times and it seems to work for me. But one more time, you cannot hide from your own mind... all outcomes will be based on the individual's efforts. I feel the whole effort of the life process is to break boundaries, experience freedom and the immensity of what and who we are. To shake ourselves from the limited identity that people have forged as a result of ignorance and live the way creation made us - utterly blissful and infinitely responsible for our lives with no boundaries, no prejudices, taking no position and with a totally inclusive mind. All boundaries and walls around us must be removed or people will block the true-life experience of who they are. The intention must be 100% pure to achieve any successful outcome.

P.S. One more time, you cannot hide from your own mind...

The whole effort of the spiritual process is to break boundaries, experience freedom and the immensity of what and who you are. To shake yourself from the limited identity that people have forged as a result of ignorance and live the way creation made you - utterly blissful and infinitely responsible for your life with no boundaries, no prejudices, taking no position and with a totally inclusive mind. All boundaries and walls around you must be removed or you will block out the true spiritual process of who you are.

The walls of self-preservation that you build today can be the walls of self-imprisonment for you tomorrow. Boundaries you've established in your life for protection will feel like constraints before too long. One part of you wants to feel safe and another part of you wants to be free. Which one is it or is it both? The good news is, you can have it all. Most people don't realise their greatness. The only thing holding people back is the way you're looking at it.

Start by removing all excuses for everything you want to have and/or do. Take this seriously and wake up to the fact that this could be your last day in life or just imagine for a moment you're 90 years old, your body is frail and you're looking back at your life. Can you see the power and opportunities you had? Can you identify how you avoided life? Every day is a great opportunity for a perfect start. Everything starts with an idea followed by an action which means moving beyond your fears. All transformation starts with little steps into the darkness of unknowing.

Accomplish one step then another and before you know it, you will be running. By removing 'Can't' from your mind and becoming a doing mind your own transformation awaits you. The unknown is always fresh, it gives us the field of infinite possibilities. As my Mum would say, "flow like a bird on the breeze". For what doesn't change, decays and dies or disease can set in. Change is the dance and rhythm of the universe as everything regularly changes, nothing stays the same. Yes, you can have a one-pointed direction and flow with the change. However, it's important to note that being detached from the outcome at the same time will bring true fulfilment to this unknown direction in life and fill you with continued amazement.

Everything in your life happens for a reason. Your responsibility is to look at these things in your life and ask this question from a positive perspective. What do I need to learn from all situations to grow? The key to creating any type of change inside requires initial activation energy to start a chain of events. Once you start there will be a chain reaction which allows you to keep going. Getting started is the hard part! It's well documented that after 3 weeks 'the change' becomes a habit and will become engrained in your central nervous system when repeated every day for only 3 weeks. Yes, the start of a life transformation. I know from personal experience that the first week is the hardest part and then things get much easier. To get a hot air balloon to take off takes the most fuel and energy at the start up stage. Avoid getting caught up in a mind trap thinking that this is the energy required throughout the entire process as this is not true. You will quickly adapt and it will become easier. Its best in the beginning to put aside the initial fear .... once again, a life choice! You and only you must make an honest decision. If you're in a place in life and you're not happy with it, you have to change something. You alone must make a conscious decision to change and it's not dependant on anyone else. It doesn't matter what others think, that is, your family, friends, society ...... they have nothing to do with it .... this decision, your life journey is yours and yours alone.

John Wheeler states nothingness is the building block of the universe. Einstein explained everything. You perceive, even your arm, your window, your wall and/or your cells, you are made up of emptiness and/or nothingness .... just condensed emptiness and that emptiness becomes condensed to make the universe as you see it. David Bone said the universe is one whole interconnected, made up of one substance, a web of interconnectedness with no divisions or boundaries, everything merging into a part of everything else. I say we are just one interconnected universal ocean. You may be thinking, what's the point? Well if there's only one substance that makes up both you and I and the entire universe and the observer cannot be separated from what they're observing, everything is just one play of one substance. To know this, make life's experience easier and simpler. There's no cause and effect, there's no karma, there's no purpose, there's no difference between you and I and/or everything else in your existence, even creation itself is all interconnected. So, whatever you thought of yourself as a separate entity - an identity, as a race, gender, a country, a religion etc., it's clear not only are you not a separate entity but you can't be separated. You are an equal part of an interconnected ocean we call a universe.

I hope you have a new awakening and think and dream the impossible. Your purpose in life is for continued improvement. This can't happen when you decide to stay the same. We must become a culture of solutions not a culture of excuses. In my home I have a poster hanging on my wall which says, 'remove can't from your mind'. I bought it many years ago and to this day it's one of my most precious possessions. So, if you want to break out of the mundane, think the impossible and make it possible, then think again. In a very short time and through new achievements, a belief in a world of endless possibilities will emerge and you'll start to realise the brilliance of yourself and life's possibilities.

Don't keep your life projects and passions built up inside as it's detrimental to your health and wellbeing. All flowers as seeds need to break through the soil to the light for them to grow and blossom. Without goals we can be used by people with goals. Make an honest list of your goals and spend every day figuring out how you can achieve these. Achieve them and make another list. Every single person is designed with capabilities, special talents and abilities. When these are developed, they enable us to accomplish anything we want in life. Every single human being is genetically structured to be great at something but how many people truly know them-selves?

A quote from Oscar Wilde: – "*It's tragic how few people ever possess their souls before they die. Nothing is rarer in any man, says Emerson, than an act of his own. This is quite true as most people are other people. Their thoughts are someone else's opinions, their life is a mimicry, their passion a quotation*".

Do something you enjoy and get great satisfaction from it .... allow no procrastination as regretfully this life's journey will be over too soon. There's no difference between you and who you consider the ultimate role model. The only difference between you and them, they've learned to use their mind and body with more power on a more consistent basis.

They've learned to manage their state of mind and control their mental focus.

Remember whatever we give one hundred per-cent focus to consistently each and every day, allowing for setbacks as learning, the mind will quickly problem solve and find solutions to achieve. The mind doesn't know the difference between imagination and reality. As we focus and imagine each day on what we want in life, this creates a neural pathway in the brain as if the experience has already occurred. This is a very powerful technique. Many people don't know how to achieve something new and all too quickly give up. By visualising yourself in this future state, yes by-passing the fears, ego, beliefs, attachments, identity's and so on, the mind and the universe will quickly find solutions to achieve whatever you imagine.

How many times in your life have you lived an entire day in a pleasant state? .... that is, blissfully, without a single moment of anxiety, agitation, irritation or stress. We now have medical and scientific evidence to show that our body and mind functions are at their best when we're in a pleasant, balanced state. Our intellectual capabilities can be almost doubled just by having a feeling of pleasantness, simply achieved by settling the internal turmoil. If your pleasantness is dependent on what's happening around you, the chance of being pleasant at all times is very slim. When we want any kind of transformation in life, it can only happen when we improve our thought patterns. The important thing to

remember is that energy has polarities of opposites ....
we can always swing the pendulum over to the other side.
When I was talking to my son about this subject, I just
called this flipping it around.

Every time there was negative conversation flowing I
asked him to flip it around and then asked him the
question again. How does it look now that you've the
power to move from negative to positive energy instantly?
All negative energy is self-created, self-defeating and
harmful to the body and mind.

Being responsible is taking ownership of your life. It's
a way of being. In the long run, we shape our lives and
we shape ourselves. The process never ends until we
pass this life experience. One of my favourite quotes is
*"The choices we make are ultimately our own
responsibility"* - Eleanor Roosevelt

Being fully responsible is to be fully conscious. Your
physical existence is possible only because of your body's
seamless ability to respond to the entire universe. Taking
absolute responsibility within yourself and around you
will start the process of you becoming the centre of any
situation. Reactivity is enslavement, responsibly is
freedom as you move yourself to an all-inclusive unit.
Your outer life may not be 100% the way you want it but
your inner life can be exactly the way you desire it by
being responsible for it. Just realise the power and
control you have for your inner world.

How you start each day is most important to get
yourself into a powerful state of mind. When you are in a
great mood you can create great results ...... you will also
set the opportunity for a great day. The better your
attitude the better you can thrive though challenges and
difficulties that come your way. Do whatever it takes to
get that feeling started.

For me I start just before daylight each day. First
thing I do is stretch my body that has been sleeping, 10-
15 min of light stretching, then breathing exercises, for

example the Wim Hof method or Chi Kung to oxygenate the cells, followed by some light meditation preparing both mind and body for the day ahead before leaving my house.

Every morning, every day of our lives we have choices to make. We have the choice to stay in bed or get up for life. It doesn't matter what you've done yesterday or years ago, it only matters what you do today to better yourself. Getting up early is not only a great gift to give yourself, to state the obvious you give yourself more life, I'm probably the laziest discipline person I know, because my mind also plays tricks on me also and sometimes I don't want to do things either but I push past that lazy mind-set.

While writing this book I realised I wasn't born with these ideas and thoughts. I self-created this new way of thinking over time and through many challenging situations and mistakes. I was the great nothing growing up in a housing estate masquerading as something, buried underneath all my own fears, insecurity's, beliefs, ego, self-doubt and lies. To move beyond all of this mess, I set about being 100% honest about everything and then spending day after day with an aim to fixing it. .... trying to get to the source of the problem, identifying these previous beliefs, ego, fears, identity's, attachments. Am I there yet? .... No is the honest answer but each day I'm one step closer in the right direction.

You'll find when you're completely truthful, the universe and life is on your side. Will it be challenging? Yes. Will it be easy? No. Will you make a lot of mistakes? Yes. Will you get hurt? Yes.

I see people afraid of trying things in life because they're afraid of getting hurt but pain is part of life's experience. This may sound upsetting for some, but pain is everywhere! It doesn't matter where you hide it will find you eventually ...... no pain no gain as they say because in challenging situations, we're more likely to grow and evolve. Challenging situations push us to make new choices. You might as well do something you love in life and help your own evolvement while doing so .... like all the great magic tricks, when the trick is revealed, you can never be fooled again and my hope is this first book reveals some of the tricks/traps in humanity for you and likewise you will never be fooled by them ever again.

Thank you for reading this book. Firstly, I'd like to thank all the people I've had the pleasure to experience in my life .... without these interactions and challenges, I wouldn't have been able to put together this book, 'Become Wise or Wounded'. The question is, do you want to become 'Wise or Wounded?' That is your choice and the greatest decision which only you can decide.

I also give great thanks to one of my greatest teachers - my Mother Joan Mangan who was fearless to live a life her own way.

I now pass on the knowledge I've accumulated. You are now the vanguard of this knowledge and consciousness which you can add to your own story and create a new wave in a vast ocean of new possibilities.

Bless you all.

To Tracy
This book has found
you, I hope you
enjoy it